D1364371

# Phonics, Phonemic Awareness, and Word Analysis for Teachers: An Interactive Tutorial

## Seventh Edition

**Robert M. Wilson**
*Professor Emeritus*
*University of Maryland*

**MaryAnne Hall**
*Georgia State University*

**Donald J. Leu, Jr.**
*University of Connecticut*

**Charles K. Kinzer**
*Vanderbilt University*

Merrill
Prentice Hall

Upper Saddle River, New Jersey
Columbus, Ohio

**Library of Congress Cataloging-in-Publication Data**

Phonics, phonemic awareness, and word analysis for teachers : an interactive tutorial /
Robert M. Wilson ... [et al.].—7th ed.
    p. cm.
  Rev. ed. of: Programmed word attack for teachers / Robert M. Wilson, MaryAnne Hall.
6th ed. c1997.
  Includes bibliographical references.
  ISBN 0-13-018171-4
  1. Word recognition. 2. Reading. 3. Reading comprehension. I. Wilson, Robert Mills.
II. Wilson, Robert Mills. Programmed word attack for teachers.

LB1050.44 .W55 2001
372.46'2—dc21                                             00-033225

**Vice President and Publisher:** Jeffrey W. Johnston
**Editor:** Linda Ashe Montgomery
**Editorial Assistant:** Jennifer Day
**Production Editor:** Mary M. Irvin
**Design Coordinator:** Diane C. Lorenzo
**Cover Design:** Bryan Huber
**Cover Art:** PhotoDisc
**Production Manager:** Pamela D. Bennett
**Editorial Production Supervision and Text Design:** Carlisle Publishers Services
**Director of Marketing:** Kevin Flanagan
**Marketing Manager:** Amy June
**Marketing Services Manager:** Krista Groshong

This book was set in Century by Carlisle Publishers Services, and was printed and bound
by Courier/Kendallville. The cover was printed by Phoenix Color Corp.

Earlier edition © 1990 by Macmillan Publishing Company. Earlier editions © 1984, 1979, 1974, and 1968 by Merrill
Publishing Company.

10 9 8 7 6
ISBN 0-13-018171-4

# Contents

# 4 Phonics: Vowels — 39

# 5 Context — 49

# 6 Sight Words — 59

# 7 Developmental Spelling Patterns — 65

# Preface

This edition marks the beginning of a new author team for this classic work. As we wrote this edition, we kept the best of the past and we added important new areas: phonological and phonemic awareness, onset and rime patterns, context, sight word knowledge, and insights made possible by knowing developmental spelling phases.

Our purpose in this edition is to provide practical information about phonemic awareness, phonics, and word analysis for preservice teacher education students and for those in-service teachers who are updating their knowledge or preparing for examinations. This self-paced tutorial allows students to learn the important aspects of phonics, phonemic awareness, and word analysis independently. As students complete their reading, they can check their understanding with "self-checks" at the end of each chapter and two separate posttests at the end of the book.

Acquiring the insights necessary for effective reading instruction requires extensive reading, study, and practice. The course time normally needed for teaching content about phonemic awareness, phonics, and word analysis included here can instead be devoted to other material. Most students go through this text on their own and then demonstrate their knowledge by passing an exam on its contents.

While we focus on phonics, phonemic awareness, and word analysis in this book, it is important to be clear about the relationship between word analysis strategies and meaning construction. Meaning must be the focus of all reading, and word analysis should be viewed as one of many strategies necessary for constructing meaning from printed language. We believe that word analysis strategies are important in a balanced program of reading, especially in the early stages, but it is also important to keep in mind that readers bring meaning to their texts as they decode the meaning in printed materials.

We feel that teachers need information about a wide range of word analysis strategies: phonological and phonemic awareness, onset and rime patterns, phonic generalizations with high utility, context use, sight word knowledge, developmental spelling phases, morphemic and structural analysis, and using a dictionary. In learning to read, children must acquire effective strategies for recognizing unfamiliar words. Each child, however, is an individual. No single strategy will meet the needs of every child in a classroom. We believe that children learn best when they have an insightful teacher who is capable of making professional judgments about what each child requires. We also believe that the information in this text will help you to develop the insights about word analysis that are so critical to children starting off successfully on their reading journeys.

After you are familiar with the content presented here, we recommend that you study procedures and materials for teaching phonics, phonemic awareness, and word analysis to students. We also recommend that you investigate diagnostic instruments that assess learners' application of reading strategies and identify the instructional needs of individuals. We recommend, too, that you keep abreast of research on this topic in order to make the *best* decisions about what to teach your students.

## CHANGES IN THIS EDITION

In this edition, we have made a number of additions, including completely new chapters on:

1. phonological awareness and phonemic awareness
2. onset and rime
3. context
4. sight words
5. developmental spelling patterns

We have also completely revised previous chapters, including the division of the phonics chapter into separate chapters on consonants and vowels. Each chapter now has a review section. We have also added two final posttests for your use. You may use one as a pretest before beginning the book or use the second posttest to provide you with an additional review experience.

## ACKNOWLEDGMENTS

We would like to thank the reviewers of our manuscript for their insights and comments: Joan B. Elliott, Indiana University of Pennsylvania; Marguerite K. Gillis, Southwest Texas State University; Peter B. Messmore, Florida Atlantic University; Karen Robinson, Otterbein University; John T. Wolinski, Salisbury State University; and Mary Lynn Woods, University of Indianapolis.

## USING THIS TEXT

Effective use of this book can best be accomplished by following these strategies:

1. Cover the answer portion of the page with a piece of paper or the marker on the inside of the back cover.
2. After you have written your answer in the appropriate blank, slide the paper down to expose the correct answer.
3. Read each frame carefully. Easy frames lead to more advanced frames that provide deeper understanding of the material.
4. Complete the review sections in each chapter as though they were tests. When you miss an item, check for the related entry in the chapter.
5. Take the final Self-Check and review as needed.

We wish you the very best in providing young children with the most important gift anyone can receive: the gift of literacy.

Donald J. Leu, Jr.  
University of Connecticut

Charles K. Kinzer  
Vanderbilt University

# Recognizing Words: Helping Children Develop Word Analysis Strategies

*1*

You are a proficient reader. When you read, you recognize most words without sounding them out. Most of the time you just think about the meaning of what you read because you recognize almost every word automatically. Your ability to recognize words rapidly and seemingly without effort is the foundation on which many other reading skills rest. How did you develop this ability?

Learning to read is a journey, the paths of which are becoming increasingly clear, especially in the early stages when learning to recognize words is an important goal. We refer to children who are just beginning their literacy journeys as "emergent readers." Emergent readers, many of whom are around the age of two to five years, are developing important oral language skills and are just beginning to consciously notice and play with the words of our language.

Supported properly by their families and insightful teachers, emergent readers will develop effective word analysis strategies that are helpful in reading. These word analysis strategies lead to accurate word recognition and, ultimately, to effective reading comprehension.

Most printed words are unfamiliar to emergent readers. At the beginning, they do not realize that printed words represent spoken words nor can they analyze printed words to determine their oral equivalent. Only gradually do they come to this insight, an important one on their literacy journey. Over time, most children develop the full range of word analysis strategies that enable them to become proficient readers, readers who are seldom conscious of these early skills that have become so automatic.

What is word analysis? Word analysis is an extensive set of knowledge about our written language and strategies that permit you to determine both the sounds of words and their meanings as you read. Word analysis develops as children acquire abilities in phonological and phonemic awareness, phonics, context use, sight word knowledge, morphemic analysis, and dictionary skills. Each contributes in important ways to help children analyze written words and determine both their sounds and their meanings. We will explore each element of word analysis in this book so that you can assist children in acquiring this important aspect of reading. We will also show you how to analyze children's developmental spelling patterns to gain insight into their developing word analysis skills.

 ## PHONOLOGICAL AWARENESS

Emergent readers gradually become aware of language as an object, something that can be analyzed and manipulated. We see this when they begin to substitute one word for another at the end of a repeated sentence, when they play rhyming games in oral language, and later when they are able to segment a spoken word like "into" into the two syllables that comprise this word. Becoming aware of language as an object that can be analyzed and manipulated is usually referred to as phonological awareness. It is an important beginning step on the way to phonemic awareness.

 ## PHONEMIC AWARENESS

Phonemes are the smallest unit of speech sounds, like the three separate sounds you hear in the word "read." Phonemic awareness is being able to hear each of these sounds as individual units. What is the difference between phonological awareness and phonemic awareness? Put simply, when you possess phonological awareness, you are aware of individual words and syllables as objects that can be analyzed and manipulated. When you possess phonemic awareness, you are aware of individual sounds or phonemes as objects that can be analyzed and manipulated. With phonological awareness you can identify the two syllables in the spoken word "into." With phonemic awareness you can hear these two syllables and you can also identify the two separate phonemes in the syllable "in" as well as the two phonemes in "to." Having phonemic awareness allows you to succeed in developing phonic knowledge because you can identify the individual sounds in words. If you cannot hear these sounds, phonics will provide little help.

 ## PHONICS

Phonics or phonic knowledge consists of two elements: (1) knowledge of the relationships between letters and sounds and (2) the ability to put together, or blend, sounds represented by letters. Letters in English do not always represent a single sound. Nevertheless, knowledge of the more regular letter-sound, or graphophonic, relationships helps us to recognize many words that we encounter while reading by permitting us to sound them out.

 ## CONTEXT USE

Using context provides important assistance during word analysis. We can often anticipate what a word is, even before we actually see it from the context that precedes the word. Or sometimes we can figure out an unfamiliar word by looking at the words and sentences that follow it. This is context use and it is an important type of word analysis skill.

 ## SIGHT WORD KNOWLEDGE

When we see a word often enough, it becomes a sight word, one we recognize instantly without having to resort to phonics or context use. High-frequency words like "me," "I," "you," children's names, and others quickly become sight words for us. As children become better readers, the set of words they know by sight, without the need to consciously analyze them, increases substantially. We seek to expand children's sight word knowledge because knowing only 200 of the most common words by sight will enable them to recognize about 50% of all the words they will encounter while reading.

## MORPHEMIC AND STRUCTURAL ANALYSIS

Morphemic analysis refers to the use of prefixes and suffixes to break a word apart for both its meaning and its pronunciation. Structural analysis refers to dividing a word into its syllables. Often, this is useful when applying phonic generalizations. Both morphemic and structural analyses are helpful in the later stages of word analysis.

## DICTIONARY SKILLS

Finally, we sometimes use a dictionary when we are trying to analyze either the pronunciation or the meaning of a word. Dictionary skills are useful for all of us.

We will explore each of these elements of word analysis in upcoming chapters. Knowing about word analysis will help children as they begin to develop proficiency in reading. You will acquire an understanding about what young children must learn in the beginning stages of their journey. This will influence your decisions about what to teach young children in order to help them become successful readers.

| | |
|---|---|
| 1. One element of reading instruction about which teachers should be familiar is word _____ . Readers use word analysis to analyze written words and to construct both their sounds and their _____ . | analysis<br><br>meanings |
| 2. Printed letters, words, and sentences are language symbols from which a reader seeks to derive _____ . Word analysis refers to those strategies a reader uses when unfamiliar words are encountered in written _____ . Both sound and meaning are _____ by the symbols in our written language. | meaning<br><br>language<br>represented |
| 3. Readers construct meaning from written language. Although emergent readers are already familiar with the spoken form of their language, most of them are unfamiliar with the _____ form of language. | written |

| | |
|---|---|
| **4.** Meaning is the most important consideration in reading. Word _____ is a tool that can help readers to obtain _____ from reading. | analysis<br><br>meaning |
| **5.** Many word _____ strategies are referred to as decoding skills. A reader must be able to use the information of the written language code in order to _____ . | analysis<br><br><br>read |
| **6.** Phonics is only one of many important word _____ strategies. Other elements of word analysis, such as phonological awareness and phonemic awareness, are skills that develop earlier. These enable readers to use word analysis _____ . | analysis<br><br><br><br>strategies |
| **7.** In reconstructing a message from written _____ , a reader uses at least three types of information. These interrelated categories are *graphophonics*, *semantics*, and *syntax*. | language |
| **8.** Grapho _____ information describes the relationship between sounds in our _____ and the written letters or spelling patterns. | phonic<br>language |
| **9.** Semantic information refers to the meaning referents of language. The vocabulary and conceptual backgrounds of a reader influence his or her ability to use _____ information. | semantic 語意學 |
| **10.** Syntax refers to the sentence patterns and structure, or grammar, of _____ . These structures, or _____ cues, are used by readers in constructing meaning from print. | language　syntactic |
| **11.** Readers use all three categories of language information simultaneously during the reading _____ . | process |
| **12.** Linguistics is the scientific study of language. Certain information from the scientific study of language, or _____ , is applicable to reading instruction. | linguistics 語言學 |

**Recognizing Words: Helping Children Develop Word Analysis　5**

| | |
|---|---|
| **13.** Phonology and phonetics, which are concerned with the study of speech sounds, are part of _____ study. Phonetics is a branch of linguistic study that deals with speech sounds and their production. *Phonics* refers to the application of information about the sounds of _____ to the teaching of reading. The term *phonics* refers to the knowledge about how _____ are represented by letters or letter combinations in written language to help readers determine the oral equivalents of words. The English language does not have a completely predictable correspondence between sounds and written _____ , thus making phonics an incomplete word analysis system. Nevertheless, relationships between letters and sounds are sufficiently predictable to make _____ a word analysis strategy that is useful when combined with other strategies. | linguistic<br><br>language<br>sounds<br><br><br><br><br>symbols<br><br><br>phonics |
| **14.** Teachers help children by teaching _____ , not phonetics. | phonics |
| **15.** Orthography is the term used to refer to the writing system of a language. The writing system, or _____ , of English is complex. English _____ is based on an alphabetic principle as well as morphological (word form) and syntactic considerations. Because of these additional influences, words are not always spelled the way they sound. | orthography<br>orthography |
| **16.** A phoneme is the smallest single unit of sound in a language that distinguishes one *morpheme* (meaning unit) from another. For example, when the words *bit* and *sit* are spoken, only the first phoneme (out of three) is different. The spoken word *at* has two _____ , whereas the spoken word cat has _____ . | phonemes     three |
| **17.** A grapheme is a written or printed representation of a phoneme, for example, the letters <u>th</u>, <u>i</u>, and <u>s</u> in the word *this*. Note that a single grapheme may include several letters when these represent a single sound. When you see the written word *at*, you see two graphemes: _____ and _____ . In the written word *path*, you see three _____ : <u>p</u>, <u>a</u>, and <u>th</u>. | a          t<br>graphemes |

| | |
|---|---|
| **18.** The written word *chat* has four letters, _____ graphemes and _____ phonemes. Two of the letters appear in a single grapheme, <u>ch</u>. This grapheme represents _____ sound. | three<br><br>three<br><br>one |
| **19.** In reading, children are expected to learn letter-sound relationships or, as they are frequently referred to, grapheme-phoneme _____ . | relationships |
| **20.** Before they learn grapheme-phoneme relationships, however, most children come to a conscious awareness of many aspects of language as discrete units, including words and syllabic units. This is often referred to as phonological _____ . | awareness |
| **21.** _____ awareness is the general term used to label this conscious awareness about the sounds of language. Phonological _____ is an important milestone for young children since it indicates that they are consciously aware of the sounds of language and can analyze and manipulate these sounds in different ways. | Phonological<br><br>awareness |
| **22.** If children can identify individual words in oral language, clap the syllables in a word, or know how to rhyme one word with another, we can be confident that they have developed _____ awareness. | phonological |
| **23.** A special aspect of phonological awareness, and a more challenging milestone, is the development of phonemic awareness. _____ awareness is demonstrated when a child can analyze and manipulate individual phonemes in oral language. Being able to identify the two sounds, or phonemes, in a spoken word like "at" would demonstrate that a child has phonemic _____ . | Phonemic<br><br><br>awareness |
| **24.** Phonemic awareness is important for children to develop because it enables them to benefit from _____ instruction. | phonics |

| | |
|---|---|
| **25.** Being able to determine the graphophonemic relationships in a word does not, by itself, always enable a reader to determine _____ . However, graphophonemic cues can be combined with other language information to result in _____ reading. | meaning<br><br>meaningful |
| **26.** A morpheme is the smallest unit of meaning in a language. The word *bookmark* has _____ morphemes. | two |
| **27.** Morphemic analysis refers to the use of meaningful parts of _____ , such as prefixes, suffixes, contractions, compounded forms, and base words, to analyze words. Structural _____ is a term often used in texts on how to teach reading to refer to what is called morphemic analysis here. In addition, structural analysis includes the study of syllabic units in words and spelling patterns influenced by the addition of affixes. | words<br><br><br>analysis |
| **28.** _____ analysis is concerned with how meaning is determined by the combination of morphemes, the smallest units of meaning in a language. | Morphemic |
| **29.** The word *box* contains one unit of meaning, or morpheme. In the word *boxes,* there are _____ morphemes: *box* and *es*. *Box* is called a free _____ since it can stand alone and another unit does not need to be added to it for the unit to have meaning. The *es* plural is an example of a bound morpheme. Bound morphemes only function when combined with a _____ morpheme. | two<br>morpheme<br><br><br><br>free |
| **30.** Morphemic analysis is an important aspect of word analysis. Use of morphemic analysis is limited, however, to words that contain identifiable morphemes, including _____ , _____ , and root words. | prefixes    suffixes |

| | |
|---|---|
| **31.** The spelling system of English is based on more than the correspondence between letters and sounds, or _____ . For example, consider word pairs such as *sane* and *sanity*, *nation* and *national*, *democracy* and *democratic*. The sounds represented by the <u>a</u> in *sane* and *sanity*, *nation* and *national*, and by the <u>o</u> in *democracy* and *democratic* are not the same, even though these word pairs contain a basic meaning unit, or _____ . Linguists use the term *morphophonemic* to refer to the combined meaning and _____ base of the English spelling system. | phonemes<br><br><br><br><br><br>morpheme<br>sound |
| **32.** Readers often use context clues during _____ analysis. Context clues require readers to rely upon the other words and the sentence patterning, or _____ , in a reading selection along with meaning cues in the material. | word<br><br>syntax |
| **33.** _____ clues provide helpful information for determining word _____ . Context cues are also helpful in determining pronunciation for readers who have heard a word before in oral language but have never seen the printed form. | Context<br>meaning |
| **34.** Efficient readers combine all _____ _____ techniques to figure out the pronunciation and _____ of unfamiliar words. | word          analysis<br>meaning |
| **35.** The ultimate aim of instruction in word analysis is to help students become more efficient readers. Efficient readers focus on meaning and recognize many words instantly. The words that readers _____ instantly comprise their sight _____ knowledge. One factor contributing to the development of extensive _____ word knowledge is a command of word analysis _____ . Extensive _____ word knowledge contributes to efficient reading. | recognize<br>word<br>sight<br>strategies<br>sight |
| **36.** In this book, we focus mostly on the _____ -phonic information. However, we do not mean to imply this is more important than the other categories. This will vary according to individual student _____ . An insightful teacher will be able to determine the strategies each child needs to develop. | grapho<br><br><br>needs |

**Recognizing Words: Helping Children Develop Word Analysis   9**

| | |
|---|---|
| **37.** Phonological awareness, phonemic awareness, phonics, context clues, sight words, structural and morphemic analyses, and use of the dictionary are word ⎯⎯⎯⎯ strategies discussed in this text. For children, this knowledge is acquired over a period of years. For you, this information is condensed into a brief, interactive tutorial to save you time. | analysis |

✔ **SELF-CHECK FOR CHAPTER ONE**

| | |
|---|---|
| **1.** Readers use word ⎯⎯⎯⎯ strategies to analyze written words in order to construct both their sounds and their meanings. Word analysis includes phonological and phonemic awareness, phonics, context use, sight word knowledge, morphemic analysis, and dictionary skills. | analysis |
| **2.** The term *graphophonic relationships* refers to the relationships between letters and ⎯⎯⎯⎯ . | sounds |
| **3.** The term *phonics* refers to the knowledge about how sounds are represented by ⎯⎯⎯⎯ . | letters |
| **4.** In English, the relationship between letters and sounds is not completely predictable. This suggests that phonics should not be the only ⎯⎯⎯⎯ analysis strategy. | word |
| **5.** A ⎯⎯⎯⎯ is the smallest single unit of sound in a language that distinguishes one morpheme from another. | phoneme |
| **6.** A ⎯⎯⎯⎯ is a written or printed representation of a phoneme. | grapheme |
| **7.** The spoken word *push* has ⎯⎯⎯⎯ phonemes. | three |
| **8.** The written word *past* has ⎯⎯⎯⎯ graphemes. | four |
| **9.** When children are able to identify individual words and syllables in a language, we can be confident that they have developed ⎯⎯⎯⎯ awareness. | phonological |

| | |
|---|---|
| **10.** When children are able to identify individual sounds, or phonemes, in a language, we can be confident that they have developed _____ awareness. | phonemic |
| **11.** A _____ is the smallest unit of meaning in a language. The word *running* has two morphemes. | morpheme |
| **12.** Readers often use surrounding words and other information, or _____ clues, during word analysis. | context |
| **13.** The words readers recognize instantly comprise their _____ word knowledge. Extensive sight word knowledge is important for efficient reading. | sight |

# The Early Stages: Phonological and Phonemic Awareness

A critical phase for emergent readers happens when they become consciously aware that language is an object, something that may be analyzed and manipulated by them in different ways: to rhyme, to play word games, and to talk about. We refer to this as phonological awareness.

What does it mean to possess phonological awareness? When young children first develop oral language, they use language to communicate and accomplish many goals that are important to them. Usually, however, they are not consciously aware of language as an abstract object that can be manipulated by them and others, taken apart and put back together in different ways, and held up for analysis. Initially, this might first happen when very young children can play the "I wanna game" with an adult. An adult initiates this word game by saying, "I wanna *banana*," attempting to get the child to imitate him or her while substituting a different noun at the end ("I wanna *apple/Suffleuppagus*/etc.") as each tries to use a sillier and sillier word until both of them end up laughing. Being able to manipulate language like this, that is, substituting a number of different words in the same slot without any intent other than to play with language, is an example of phonological awareness. Another example of phonological awareness takes place when children can clap or tap each word in a sentence as they say it, indicating their awareness of individual words that actually occur in oral language as a continuous stream of sound. Phonological awareness also exists when a child can clap or tap each syllable in a sentence or word ("I want a ba-na-na."). When children achieve phonological awareness, they are aware of language as an object, something that can be analyzed and manipulated. This is an important first step in their journey to develop word analysis skills and reading ability.

A very important next step happens when young children begin to hear the separate sounds of a language, not just the words or the syllables. This is the beginning of a special aspect of phonological awareness, phonemic awareness, and a critical stage in a child's literacy journey. The term "phoneme" means the smallest unit of speech sound. Phonemic awareness occurs when children become aware of individual phonemes in our language and can manipulate them in different ways. We see evidence of this important milestone when children develop the ability to rhyme one word with another (cat – pat). Being able to play a rhyming game with someone else indicates phonemic awareness because a child is manipulating individual phonemes at the beginning of words. Phonemic awareness also includes the ability to put several sounds together to form a single word. When you give a child several sounds (/k/–/at/) and he or she can blend them together to form an oral word ("cat"), we know that the child has developed phonemic awareness. Later this will be essential for developing word analysis skills with written language such as phonic knowledge.

Many people use the terms "phonological analysis" and "phonemic analysis" interchangeably. Some use the term "phonemic analysis" to capture both phases in a child's development. We prefer the more precise use of the separate terms. We use the term "phonological analysis" to refer to conscious awareness of oral language as an object at the *word* and *syllable* level. We use the term "phonemic analysis" to refer to the conscious awareness of oral language as an object at the individual *phoneme* level. Phonological awareness is important because it gets the word "analysis" ball rolling as children begin to look at our language in an analytical manner. Phonemic awareness is important because it means that children are capable of analyzing the individual *sounds* of our language. This is essential to the successful development of phonic knowledge and an understanding of the alphabetic principle, which are important aspects of word analysis.

| | |
|---|---|
| 1. Two aspects of oral language development that are important for developing word analysis skills and reading are _____ awareness and _____ awareness. | phonological phonemic |
| 2. Phonological awareness and phonemic awareness are important for developing the ability to _____ . | read |
| 3. Definitions of phonological awareness and phonemic awareness differ among educators. Nevertheless, a common element in all definitions is that children who possess these abilities are consciously aware of language as an _____ that can be manipulated by them and others and held up for analysis. | object |
| 4. In this book, we refer to _____ analysis to mean the conscious awareness of language as an object at the word and syllable level. | phonological |
| 5. We refer to _____ analysis to mean the conscious awareness of language as an object at the individual sound, or phonemic, level. | phonemic |
| 6. In oral language, being able to break up a word like *dog* into the separate sound elements /d/, /o/, and /g/ would demonstrate a high level of _____ awareness. | phonemic |
| 7. Being able to break up a sentence into its constituent words would be a demonstration of _____ awareness. | phonological |
| 8. Being able to identify the initial consonant sound in a word like *put* would be an example of _____ awareness. | phonemic |
| 9. When a child is able to rhyme words, we know that the child has developed an aspect of _____ awareness. | phonemic |
| 10. Being able to clap or tap each syllable in a word like *table* would demonstrate _____ awareness. | phonological |
| 11. When a child is able to blend together the oral elements of a word like *book*, we can say the child has developed an important aspect of _____ awareness. | phonemic |

**The Early Stages: Phonological and Phonemic Awareness       15**

| | |
|---|---|
| **12.** Usually, _____ awareness develops before _____ awareness. | phonological    phonemic |
| **13.** The relationship between phonological/phonemic awareness and reading/writing is not unidirectional. Many children develop or enhance their phonological/phonemic awareness from their _____ experiences. They become more aware of language units like words and phonemes from their interactions with print. | reading/writing |
| **14.** How do phonological and phonemic awareness work to help children become better readers and writers? First, being able to analyze oral language is likely to make it easier for children to think analytically about _____ language. | written |
| **15.** Second, analyzing the separate sounds in our language when phonemic awareness is achieved is likely to make it easier for children to match letters with _____ , the content of phonics. | sounds |
| **16.** Third, phonemic awareness supports children in developing an awareness of the alphabetic principle, that is, _____ in our written language often represent sounds in a reasonably consistent manner. | letters |
| **17.** Research indicates that phonemic awareness in kindergarten appears to be the best single predictor of successful reading acquisition. This means that the extent to which children accomplish _____ awareness in kindergarten predicts reasonably well their ability to learn to read in later grades. | phonemic |
| **18.** While this is a powerful finding, it is not yet clear to what extent phonemic awareness causes success in reading or to what extent success in reading causes high levels of phonemic awareness. It is clear that learning to _____ is likely also to assist the development of phonemic awareness. | read |
| **19.** Phonemic awareness is not phonics even though it makes the development of phonic knowledge easier. Phonemic awareness takes place in _____ language. Phonics takes place in written language. | oral |

| | |
|---|---|
| **20.** Most children, about 80 percent, develop _____ awareness by the middle of the first grade. | phonemic |
| **21.** The remaining 20 percent of children often find it challenging to learn to _____ . | read |
| **22.** A logical outcome of this analysis of phonological awareness and phonemic awareness is that play with oral _____ should be included in a broad program of early literacy development for young children in kindergarten and in preschool. These games would include nursery rhymes, word and sound riddles, songs, and poems. Teachers also use read aloud books that manipulate the sounds of spoken language. | language |
| **23.** Phonemic awareness is not a single developmental milestone. Instead, it is a gradual process of an increasing ability to manipulate the _____ of language in different ways. | sounds |
| **24.** Rhyming ability, for example, appears much _____ than the ability to separate out each of the separate sounds in a word like "dog." | earlier |
| **25.** One of the later abilities to develop is the ability to blend together separate _____ in order to construct a word like "cat." | phonemes |
| **26.** It is clear than phonemic awareness contributes in important ways to the development of early _____ skills. | reading |

✔ **SELF-CHECK FOR CHAPTER TWO**

| | |
|---|---|
| **1.** The conscious awareness of language as an object at the individual sound, or phonemic, level is important to later reading success. We refer to this as _____ awareness. | phonemic |
| **2.** Being able to identify individual words and syllables in spoken language is referred to as _____ awareness. | phonological |
| **3.** _____ awareness usually develops before _____ awareness. | Phonological    phonemic |

| | |
|---|---|
| **4.** A close relationship between the letters and sounds in a language is referred to as the _____ principle. | alphabetic |
| **5.** In kindergarten, the best single predictor of later reading success is a child's level of _____ awareness. | phonemic |
| **6.** Phonemic awareness takes place in _____ language. Phonics instruction takes place in _____ language. | oral<br>written |
| **7.** Phonemic awareness is likely to assist in the development of _____ , but the development of reading is also likely to extend a child's _____ awareness. | reading<br>phonemic |
| **8.** About _____ percent of children develop phonemic awareness by the middle of the first grade. | 80 |
| **9.** Being able to tap the syllables in a word would be an example of _____ awareness. | phonological |
| **10.** Achieving phonemic awareness is likely to make it _____ for children to learn phonics. | easier |

# Phonics: Onset, Rime, and Consonant Patterns

Letter-sound relationships in English are somewhat predictable and rule-governed. The fact that many letters in English map reasonably well onto sounds is referred to as the *alphabetic principle*. The alphabetic principle is important for readers to recognize. In English, not all letters map as perfectly to sounds the way they might in other languages such as Spanish. Nevertheless, the patterns that do exist in English provide important information for children when they encounter an unfamiliar word.

Understanding the patterns that relate letters to sounds is often referred to as phonics or phonic knowledge. Phonic knowledge and phonic strategies are important to word analysis. Being able to determine the oral equivalent of a written word by sounding it out helps children to determine its meaning.

Initial phonics instruction often begins by teaching children common onset and rime patterns. Onset patterns include initial consonant letters found at the *beginning* of syllables and words such as <u>b</u>, <u>c</u>, <u>d</u>, <u>f</u>, <u>g</u>, <u>sn</u>, <u>st</u>, or <u>str</u>. Rime patterns include a limited set of the most common *endings* to syllables and words such as -<u>ake</u>, -<u>ack</u>, -<u>ail</u>, or -<u>ame</u>. By combining onset and rime patterns, children can quickly begin to apply the alphabetic principle to unlock the sounds of many written words, for example, bake, cake, fake, snake, stake, back, snack, stack, and so on. Onset and rime patterns are often an early component of phonics instruction. It is easier for children to use onset and rime patterns since they only need to sound out two elements, not the many elements that might be required if they had to sound out long strings of letters in words such as *afternoon*.

As children develop a greater understanding of the alphabetic principle, they are often taught other elements, including additional consonant patterns and vowel patterns. This chapter will cover onset and rime patterns as well as several additional consonant patterns, including consonant clusters, special consonant patterns, and silent consonant patterns. The next chapter will cover vowel patterns.

## ONSET: INITIAL CONSONANT LETTERS

| | |
|---|---|
| **1.** Linguistically, consonants are sounds produced by a restriction in the airstream. In English, single consonants contain the most consistent relationship between letters and _____ . | sounds |
| **2.** Thus, onset patterns of initial consonants, combined with preparation in common rime patterns, are almost always included during beginning _____ instruction. Even teachers who teach few phonic generalizations will help their students to develop an understanding of letter-sound relationships for single _____ appearing in the _____ position. | reading<br><br><br>consonants    onset |
| **3.** Consonants also carry more information about words than _____ as seen in the following examples. The first sentence is missing all of the vowels. The second sentence is missing all of the consonants. Try to complete the missing letters in each sentence below, one containing only vowels and one containing only consonants. Which sentence is the easiest to complete?<br>(a) _ _ e _ _ _ o _ e _ i _ e  o _  _ o _ _ o _ a _ _ _ !<br>(b) S p _ n d  m _ r _  t _ m _  _ n  c _ n s _ n _ n t s!<br>The _____ sentence is the easiest to complete. | vowels<br><br><br><br><br><br>second |
| **4.** Letter-sound relationships for onset consonants are often taught with "key-word charts" of memorable words beginning with each of the initial _____ . | consonants |

**5.** The word *bell* is the key word for the onset consonant _____ .

The word *cake* is the key word for the onset consonant _____ .

The word *duck* is the key word for the onset consonant _____ .

The word *fish* is the key word for the onset consonant _____ .

The word *goat* is the key word for the onset consonant _____ .

The word *hill* is the key word for the onset consonant _____ .

The word *jump* is the key word for the onset consonant _____ .

The word *kite* is the key word for the onset consonant _____ .

The word *light* is the key word for the onset consonant _____ .

The word *mail* is the key word for the onset consonant _____ .

The word *nail* is the key word for the onset consonant _____ .

The word *pan* is the key word for the onset consonant _____ .

The word *rug* is the key word for the onset consonant _____ .

The word *sock* is the key word for the onset consonant _____ .

The word *turtle* is the key word for the onset consonant _____ .

The word *valentine* is the key word for the onset consonant _____ .

The word *wagon* is the key word for the onset consonant _____ .

The word *yellow* is the key word for the onset consonant _____ .

The word *zebra* is the key word for the onset consonant _____ .

b

c

d

f

g

h

j

k

l

m

n

p

r

s

t

v

w

y

z

**6.** These _____ consonants are included in beginning phonics instruction.

onset

 **RIME**

Table 1 shows the most common rime patterns. These patterns, along with initial consonants and consonant combinations are often included in the early part of phonics programs. Knowing these rime patterns helps young readers to unlock the pronunciation of many words that they encounter.

**Table 1.**

The Thirty-Seven Most Common Rime Patterns

| -a | -e | -i | -o | -u |
|---|---|---|---|---|
| back | meat | nice | clock | duck |
| mail | bell | stick | joke | rug |
| rain | crest | wide | shop | jump |
| cake | | light | store | junk |
| sale | | ill | not | |
| game | | win | | |
| plan | | line | | |
| bank | | bring | | |
| trap | | think | | |
| crash | | trip | | |
| cat | | fit | | |
| plate | | | | |
| saw | | | | |
| stay | | | | |

This table is based on work initially conducted by Wylie and Durrell (1970).

**7.** From Table 1, we can see that the most frequent rime patterns begin with the vowel letter _____ and the least frequent rime patterns begin with the vowel _____ .

a

e

**8.** Two words that use the -ake rime pattern, begin with a single consonant, and are likely to be familiar to many first graders from their oral vocabulary would include _____ and _____ .

bake, cake, fake, Jake, lake, make, rake, take, or wake

| | |
|---|---|
| **9.** Two words that use the -<u>ot</u> rime pattern, begin with a single consonant, and are likely to be familiar to many first graders from their oral vocabulary would include _____ and _____ . | got, hot, lot, not, pot, or rot |
| **10.** Rime patterns do not only appear in _____ words, they also appear in multiple syllable words such as <u>light</u>-<u>ning</u>. | one-syllable |
| **11.** Thus, rime patterns are very helpful when decoding both _____ and words. | syllables |
| **12.** You will discover many different labels used for rime patterns. These include terms such as "phonograms" and "word families." Each term refers to common patterns containing a vowel and any following consonants within a _____ . | syllable |

## CONSONANT PATTERNS

### Consonant Clusters

| | |
|---|---|
| **13.** We have looked at initial consonants appearing in the _____ position. We should also recognize that multiple consonants might appear together at the beginning of words and syllables. These are called *consonant clusters*. <u>Consonant clusters include two or three _____ that often appear together, such as <u>ch</u>, <u>th</u>, <u>st</u>, <u>str</u>, <u>bl</u>, or <u>pr</u>.</u> | onset<br><br>consonants |
| **14.** There are two different types of consonant _____ that appear in the onset position (at the beginning) of words and syllables: consonant digraphs and consonant blends. | clusters |

### Consonant Digraphs

| | |
|---|---|
| **15.** Consonant digraphs are two different consonant _____ that appear together and represent a single sound, or phoneme, not usually associated with either letter, for example, <u>ch</u> (child), <u>ph</u> (phone), <u>sh</u> (shop), and <u>th</u> (thin). | letters |

| | |
|---|---|
| **16.** Can you identify the consonant digraphs in the following key words? These are the most common consonant digraphs. The word *white* is the key word for the consonant digraph _____ . | |
| | wh |
| The word *chair* is the key word for the consonant digraph _____ . | ch |
| The words *this* and *thin* are the key words for the consonant digraph _____ . | th |
| The word *shop* is the key word for the consonant digraph _____ . | sh |
| The word *phone* is the key word for the consonant digraph _____ . | ph |
| **17.** The most common consonant digraphs appearing in the onset position include _____ , _____ , _____ , _____ , and _____ . | wh   ch   th sh   ph |
| **18.** The consonant _____ th and ch have several sounds often associated with each. | digraphs |
| **19.** Let's look at the consonant digraph th. This digraph represents two different sounds: the voiced and voiceless th sound. Pronounce the words *this*, *that*, *their*, and *them*. The digraph _____ in these words is called the voiced th sound since we add voice to it when we say it. (Put your hand on your throat as you say each word and you may feel the vibration of the voicing.) | th |
| **20.** Pronounce the words *think* and *thin*. Hold one hand on your throat and you will not feel any voicing. The beginning sound in these words is _____ . We call it the unvoiced, or voiceless, _____ . | different th |
| **21.** The phoneme represented by th in *this* is the _____ th sound; the phoneme represented by th in *thin* is the unvoiced _____ sound. | voiced th |

| | |
|---|---|
| **22.** As you pronounce the following words, indicate whether the <u>th</u> digraph in them is voiced or unvoiced. | |
| thank _____ | unvoiced |
| the _____ | voiced |
| thermos _____ | unvoiced |
| thumb _____ | unvoiced |
| these _____ | voiced |
| **23.** Now, let's look at the digraph <u>ch</u>. This consonant digraph represents three different sounds: the sound of _____ as in *chair*, the sound of _____ as in *character*, and the sound of _____ as in *chef*. | ch<br><br>k<br><br>sh |
| **24.** Pronounce the words *character* and *chorus*. These words begin with the sound usually associated with the letter _____ . <u>Ch</u> sometimes represents the sound associated with<br><br>_____ . | k<br><br><br><br>k |
| **25.** Say the words *chef* and *chiffon*. These words begin with the sound usually associated with the digraph _____ . *Chef*, *chiffon*, and *shoe* all sound the _____ in the onset position. | sh<br>same |
| **26.** Let's summarize what we know about consonant digraphs appearing in the onset position. A consonant digraph is composed of _____ consonant letters that represent a single _____ . Consonant digraphs include: _____ , _____ , _____ , _____ , and _____ . The onset digraph _____ may be voiced, as in *this*, or voiceless, as in *thin*. The onset digraph _____ may represent three different phonemes: the sounds often associated with <u>ch</u>, <u>k</u>, and <u>sh</u>. | two<br>phoneme    wh<br>ch    th    sh    ph<br>th<br>ch |
| **27.** Look at these words: *picture*, *phone*, and *pleasure*. Only one of these words has a consonant digraph in the onset position. That word is _____ . | phone |

## 📖📖 Consonant Blends

| | |
|---|---|
| **28.** A second type of consonant cluster appearing at the onset position is called a consonant _____ . A consonant blend consists of two or three consecutive consonant letters, each representing a separate phoneme that is blended together. | blend |
| **29.** Here are several examples of consonant blends: <u>br</u>ick, <u>bl</u>ue, <u>scr</u>eam, <u>sk</u>ip, and <u>str</u>eet. Notice how you can hear elements of each of the separate _____ as they are blended together. | phonemes |
| **30.** Identify the consonant blends in the onset position for these key words.<br><br>The word *blue* is the key word for the consonant blend _____ .<br><br>The word *clown* is the key word for the consonant blend _____ .<br><br>The word *flower* is the key word for the consonant blend _____ .<br><br>The word *glove* is the key word for the consonant blend _____ .<br><br>The word *plane* is the key word for the consonant blend _____ .<br><br>The word *sleep* is the key word for the consonant blend _____ .<br><br>The word *splash* is the key word for the consonant blend _____ .<br><br>All of these consonant blends end with _____ . Because of this, they are sometimes called the _____ blends. | bl<br><br>cl<br><br>fl<br><br>gl<br><br>pl<br><br>sl<br><br>spl<br>l<br>"l" |
| **31.** Now, look at these key words and identify the consonant blends in the onset position.<br><br>The word *bread* is the key word for the consonant blend _____ .<br><br>The word *crack* is the key word for the consonant blend _____ .<br><br>The word *drum* is the key word for the consonant blend _____ . | br<br><br>cr<br><br>dr |

The word *frog* is the key word for the consonant blend

_____ .

fr

The word *green* is the key word for the consonant blend

_____ .

gr

The word *princess* is the key word for the consonant blend

_____ .

pr

The word *tree* is the key word for the consonant blend

_____ .

tr

The word *three* is the key word for the consonant blend

_____ .

thr

All of these consonant _____ end with _____ .
Because of this, they are sometimes called the _____
blends.

blends    r
"r"

**32.** Now, look at these key words and identify the consonant
blends in the onset position.
The word *scale* is the key word for the consonant blend

_____ .

sc

The word *skate* is the key word for the consonant blend

_____ .

sk

The word *sled* is the key word for the consonant blend

_____ .

sl

The word *smoke* is the key word for the consonant blend

_____ .

sm

The word *snail* is the key word for the consonant blend

_____ .

sn

The word *spoon* is the key word for the consonant blend

_____ .

sp

The word *stamp* is the key word for the consonant blend

_____ .

st

The word *swim* is the key word for the consonant blend

_____ .

sw

The word *screen* is the key word for the consonant blend

_____ .

scr

The word *spring* is the key word for the consonant blend

_____ .

spr

The word *squirrel* is the key word for the consonant blend

_____ .

squ

| | |
|---|---|
| The word *string* is the key word for the consonant blend _____ . | str |
| All of these consonant blends _____ with _____. Because of this, they are sometimes called the _____ blends. | begin   s  "s" |

**33.** The three main categories of _____ blends are (1) those with _____ as the final letter, (2) those with _____ as the beginning letter, and (3) those with _____ as the final letter. | consonant  l  s  r |

**34.** As you have just learned, a consonant _____ is a combination of two or three _____ letters, each of which retains its own _____ when pronounced. | blend  consonant  phoneme (sound) |

## Special Consonant Patterns

**35.** The following _____ letters can represent more than one sound when they appear in certain contexts: $\underline{c}$, g, $\underline{s}$, $\underline{q}$, $\underline{d}$, $\underline{x}$, $\underline{t}$, and $\underline{z}$. Many of these patterns are presented in reading programs when _____ is taught. As a result, we will cover them here. | consonant

phonics |

**36.** First, let's take a look at the single onset consonants $\underline{c}$ and g since they follow a similar pattern. Look at the two lists below and see if you can determine the two sounds of $\underline{c}$ in the onset position.

| List A | List B |
|--------|--------|
| come   | city   |
| cow    | celery |
| capture| cycle  |
| cut    | cymbal |

The words in List A all begin with the same sound. The sound in the onset position in List A is called the "hard c" sound; this sound is often represented by the letter _____ in words like *kite*. Notice, too, the three vowel letters that follow $\underline{c}$ in each of the words in List A. These vowel letters are _____ , _____ , and _____ .

(right column for 36:)
k

o

a   u

| | |
|---|---|
| **37.** Now, let's look at a few other words beginning with the letter <u>c</u> and followed by the vowel letter <u>o</u>, <u>a</u> or <u>u</u>: _comb_, _cone_, _cat_, _can_, _cucumber_, and _cute_. These words also follow the pattern since the onset letter <u>c</u> is pronounced like the _____ sound when followed by the vowel letters _____ , _____ , or _____ . We refer to this as the "_____ c" sound. | k<br><br>o<br><br>a   u<br>hard |
| **38.** The words in List B all begin with what we call the "soft c" sound. This is the sound represented by the letter <u>s</u> in words like _sale_. Notice the three _____ letters that follow <u>c</u> in each of the words in List B. These vowel letters are _____ , _____ , and _____ . | vowel<br>i<br>e   y |
| **39.** Now, let's look at a few other words beginning with the letter <u>c</u> followed by the vowel letter <u>i</u>, <u>e</u>, or <u>y</u>: _circle_, _circus_, _center_, _cent_, _cylinder_, and _cypress_. These words also follow this pattern since the onset letter <u>c</u> is pronounced like the _____ sound when it is followed by the vowel letters _____ , _____ , or _____ . We refer to this as the "_____ c" sound. | /s/<br>i<br>e   y<br>soft |
| **40.** You can see that the letter-sound relationship for the onset letter <u>c</u> is fairly regular. The pronunciation of this letter is usually determined by the _____ letter that follows it. | vowel |
| **41.** Now we can state the rule about letter-sound relationships that is often true for the onset letter c. The onset letter <u>c</u> usually represents the sound associated with the letter <u>k</u> when it is followed by the vowel letters _____ , _____ , and _____ . We refer to this as the "_____ c" sound. The onset letter <u>c</u> usually represents the sound associated with <u>s</u> when it is followed by the vowel letters _____ , _____ , and _____ . We refer to this as the "_____ c" sound. | o<br>a   u<br>hard<br><br>e<br>y   i<br>soft |

**42.** The onset consonant letter g has a letter-sound relationship that patterns itself just like the letter c. Look at the two lists below and see if you can determine the two sounds of g in the onset position.

| List A | List B |
|--------|--------|
| good | gentle |
| goat | gem |
| game | gym |
| gun | giraffe |

The words in List A all begin with the sound most commonly associated with the onset consonant g. This is called the "hard g" sound. Notice the three vowel letters that follow g in each of the words in List A. These vowel letters are _____ , _____ , and _____ .

o

a    u

**43.** Now, let's look at a few other words beginning with the letter g and followed by the vowel letter o, a, or u: *go, gone, gate, gas, guppy,* and *guy.* These words also follow the pattern since the onset letter g is pronounced like the _____ sound when it is followed by the vowel letters _____ , _____ , or _____ . We refer to this as the " _____ g" sound.

g

o    a

u    hard

**44.** The words in List B all begin with what we call the "soft g" sound. This is the sound represented by the letter j in words like *jam.* Notice the three _____ letters that follow g in each of the words in List B. These vowel letters are _____ , _____ , and _____ .

vowel

e

y    i

**45.** Now, let's look at a few other words beginning with the letter g followed by the vowel letter i, e, or y: *germ, giant, genius, gypsy,* and *gyrate.* These words also follow this pattern since the onset letter g is pronounced like the _____ sound when it is followed by the vowel letters _____ , _____ , or _____ . We refer to this as the " _____ g" sound.

j

i    e

y    soft

**46.** Now we can state the rule about the letter-sound relationships that is often true for the onset letter _____ .

g

| | |
|---|---|
| The onset letter g usually represents the sound associated with g when it is followed by the vowel letters _____ , _____ , and _____ . We refer to this as the " _____ g" sound. | o<br>a  u<br>hard |
| The onset letter g usually represents the sound associated with the letter j when it is followed by the vowel letters _____ , _____ , and _____ . We refer to this as the " _____ g" sound. | i<br>e  y<br>soft |

47. <u>S</u> is another consonant _____ that has letter-sound relationships that pattern themselves in somewhat regular ways. The sound most commonly associated with <u>s</u> is represented by the <u>s</u> in the key word *sock*.

letter

   Pronounce the words *runs*, *his*, and *boys*. What letter usually represents the last sound that you hear in these words?

   _____

z

   The use of the letter <u>s</u> to represent the sound associated with the letter <u>z</u> is not taught as often as is the more common letter-sound association for <u>s</u> because <u>s</u> is more _____ in the onset position. In the case of plurals or verb forms where <u>s</u> appears at the end of words, there are usually context or word-form clues that make knowing the letter-sound association less important.

common

48. The <u>s</u> appearing in the _____ position in words like *sun*, *sit*, or *sing* represents the most common sound for this letter.

onset

49. The <u>s</u> appearing at the end of words like *his*, *runs*, and *boys* represents the sound often associated with the letter _____ .

z

50. Complete the following generalizations related to the sounds represented by the letter <u>s</u>:

   When the letter <u>s</u> appears in the _____ position, it represents the most common sound for <u>s</u>, the sound that appears at the beginning of the word *sun*.

onset

   When <u>s</u> appears at the _____ of a word, it represents one of two sounds, either the sound usually associated with the letter _____ or the sound usually represented by the letter _____ .

end

s

z

| | |
|---|---|
| **51.** <u>T</u> is another consonant letter that represents several different _____ . You know that the sound represented by the letter <u>t</u> is the sound heard in the key word *turtle*. However, in combination with certain other letters, <u>t</u> can represent other sounds. | sounds |
| **52.** Pronounce the words *celebration*, *location*, and *vacation*. What are the last four letters in each word? _____ | tion |
| **53.** Complete the following generalization: <br><br> In the suffix _____ , the letter <u>t</u> represents the sound of the digraph _____ . | tion <br> sh |
| **54.** Now, look at another pattern for <u>t</u>. Pronounce the words *virtue*, *virtuous*, and *mutual*. The sound represented by <u>t</u> in these words is usually associated with the letters _____ . In each case, the letter following <u>t</u> is _____ . | ch <br> u |
| **55.** Complete the following generalization: <br><br> When the letter <u>t</u> is followed by the letter _____ , it sometimes represents the sound associated with the consonant digraph _____ . | u <br><br> ch |
| **56.** <u>X</u> is another consonant letter that represents several sounds. The common sound associated with the letter <u>x</u> is the same sound heard at the end of the word *books*. Thus, it can be said that the most common sound for the letter <u>x</u> represents the sounds associated with the letters _____ . | ks |
| **57.** Pronounce the words *exist*, *examine*, and *exhibit*. The letter _____ in these words represents the sounds associated with the letters <u>gz</u>. | x |
| **58.** Here is another sound that the letter <u>x</u> sometimes represents. Pronounce the words *xylophone* and *xenon*. What letter usually represents the sound associated with <u>x</u> in these words? _____ Where is the <u>x</u> in *xylophone* and *xenon*? _____ | z <br> onset (at the beginning) |

| | |
|---|---|
| **59.** Complete the following generalization:<br><br>When the letter <u>x</u> appears in the _____ position, it usually represents the sound associated with _____ . | onset<br><br>z |
| **60.** The common sound associated with <u>d</u> is heard in the key word *dog.* Say the words gra<u>d</u>ual, e<u>d</u>ucate, and indivi<u>d</u>ual. The letter _____ usually represents the sound of the underlined letter. The letter _____ follows the underlined <u>d</u> in each word. | j<br><br>u |
| **61.** Complete the following generalization:<br><br>When <u>d</u> is followed by the vowel _____ , it sometimes represents the sound associated with the letter _____ . | u<br><br>j |

## Silent Consonant Patterns

| | |
|---|---|
| **62.** You have learned that some consonant letters represent more than one _____ . You should also know that there are situations in which consonant letters do not represent sounds, but instead, they serve as markers for certain language patterns. The common terminology is *silent letter.* However, no letters really have sounds; letters merely represent sounds. | sound |
| **63.** Look at the words *tall, off,* and *miss.*<br>In each of the words, there is a _____ consonant.<br>In the spoken word *tall,* there is _____ /l/ sound.<br>In the spoken word *off,* there is _____ /f/ sound.<br>In the spoken word *miss,* there is _____ /s/ sound. | double<br>one<br>one<br>one |
| **64.** Complete the following generalization:<br>When there is a double consonant in a word, usually only _____ of the consonants is heard. | one |
| **65.** Pronounce the words *knife, know,* and *knight.* What letter usually represents the first sound in these words? _____<br>The first two letters in each of the words are _____ .<br>Because <u>k</u> is _____ , it can be called a _____ in this spelling pattern. | n<br><br>kn<br>silent    silent letter (or a marker) |

**66.** Complete the following generalization:

When a word or syllable starts with the letters <u>kn</u>, the

_____ is _____ .

Pronounce the words *gnat*, *gnaw*, and *gnome*. What letter usually represents the first sound in these words? _____

The first two letters in each of the words are _____ .

The g is _____ , or a marker, in this _____ pattern.

| | |
|---|---|
| k | silent (or a marker) |
| n | |
| gn | |
| silent | spelling |

**67.** Complete the following generalization:

When a word or syllable starts with the letters <u>gn</u>, the

_____ is _____ .

| | |
|---|---|
| g | silent (or a marker) |

**68.** Pronounce the words *wrong*, *write*, and *wreath*. The letter that represents the first sound in these words is _____ .

What letter is silent (or a marker)? _____

When a word or syllable starts with <u>wr</u>, the _____ is silent, or a marker.

| |
|---|
| r |
| w |
| w |

**69.** In the preceding examples, three consonant combinations that contain a silent letter or marker are _____ , _____ , and _____ . In each of these letter combinations, the first of the two consonants is _____ .

| | |
|---|---|
| kn | gn |
| wr | |
| silent (or a marker) | |

**70.** Pronounce the words *dumb*, *climb*, and *comb*. What letter represents the final sound in these words? _____

What letter follows the <u>m</u>? _____

Does <u>b</u> represent a sound? (yes or no) _____

| |
|---|
| m |
| b |
| no |

**71.** Complete the following generalization:

When <u>b</u> is preceded by <u>m</u>, the _____ is _____ , or a marker.

| | |
|---|---|
| b | silent |

**72.** Look at the words *doubt* and *debt*. What are the last two letters?

_____

Which of the last two letters is silent, or a marker? _____

| |
|---|
| bt |
| b |

| | |
|---|---|
| **73.** Complete the following generalization:<br><br>When the letters <u>bt</u> appear together, the _____ is silent, <u>or a marker.</u> | b |
| **74.** Letter combinations in which <u>b</u> does not represent a sound are _____ and _____ . | mb     bt |
| **75.** Look at the words *high, might,* and *fight.* What three consecutive letters do you see in each of the above words? _____<br>Pronounce each word. What letter represents the last sound in *high?* _____ | igh<br><br>i |
| **76.** Complete the following generalization:<br><br>When the letters <u>igh</u> appear together, the _____ and the _____ are usually _____ and the vowel has a long <u>i sound.</u> | g<br><br>h     silent (or a marker) |
| **77.** Look at the words *fetch, itch,* and *catch.* What three consecutive letters do you see in each of these words? _____<br>Pronounce each word. Which of the three letters in the <u>tch</u> combination does not represent a sound? _____ | tch<br><br>t |
| **78.** Complete the following generalization:<br><br>When the letters <u>tch</u> appear together, the letter _____ is <u>usually</u> _____ . | t<br>silent (a marker) |
| **79.** In addition to the generalizations stated previously, there are other situations in which consonant letters do not represent sounds. The following words illustrate some other examples of consonant letters that do not represent sounds. Pronounce each word and indicate the consonant that does not represent a sound:<br><br>*whole* _____<br>*hour* _____<br>*khaki* _____<br>*rhubarb* _____<br>*folk* _____<br>*calm* _____<br>*psychology* _____<br>*island* _____ | <br><br><br><br><br><br>w<br>h<br>h<br>h<br>l<br>l<br>p<br>s |

| | |
|---|---|
| **80.** Letters in English do not always represent a single _____ ; nevertheless, knowledge of the more regular letter-sound relationships helps us to recognize many of the _____ we encounter. Understanding the basic elements of phonic knowledge is especially important for teachers of beginning readers. | sound<br><br>words |

✔ **SELF-CHECK FOR CHAPTER THREE**

| | |
|---|---|
| **1.** In English, the most consistent letter-sound relationships occur with _____ . | consonants |
| **2.** Onset patterns appear at the _____ of words or syllables and consist of _____ . | beginning<br>consonants |
| **3.** Rime patterns appear at the _____ of syllables or words and begin with a _____ . | end<br>vowel |
| **4.** Onset and rime patterns combine to form _____ or _____ . | words,<br>syllables |
| **5.** Consonant clusters include two or three consonant letters that appear _____ . | together |
| **6.** The letters <u>ch</u> in the word *choose* are called a consonant _____ since they are two consecutive consonant letters that represent a _____ sound, not usually associated with either letter. | digraph<br>single |
| **7.** The letters <u>sk</u> in the word *skip* are called a consonant _____ since they are two consecutive consonant letters, each representing a separate _____ that is blended together with the other. | blend<br>phoneme |
| **8.** The onset letter <u>c</u> usually represents the sound associated with the letter <u>k</u> when it is followed by the vowel letters _____ , _____ , and _____ . We refer to this as the "_____ c" sound. | a<br>o    u<br>hard |

| | |
|---|---|
| **9.** The onset letter g usually represents the sound associated with the letter j when it is followed by the vowel letters _____ , _____ , and _____ . We refer to this as the "_____ g" sound. | e<br>i   y<br>soft |
| **10.** When there is a double consonant in a word, usually only one of the consonants is heard. The other is _____ . | silent (or a marker) |
| **11.** When a word or syllable starts with the letters <u>kn</u>, <u>gn</u>, or <u>wr</u>, the _____ letter is usually _____ . | first   silent (or a marker) |

以發音為主的教學
方法

# Phonics: Vowels

The following discussion of the letter-sound relationships that exist for vowels continues our exploration of phonic knowledge. The first section will explore letter-sound relationships between single vowels and vowel clusters. The second section will explore several generalizations that help to explain the patterning of letter-sound relationships for vowels. These relationships are often determined by where, in a word, a vowel appears. You will discover that the position of a vowel within a spelling pattern often provides more cues about its sound than does knowledge about letter-sound relationships. Regional speech patterns also influence the pronunciation of vowel phonemes.

1. Vowels are sounds produced without a restriction in the airstream. There are five letters that are often associated with vowel sounds: <u>a</u>, <u>e</u>, _____ , _____ , and _____ . In addition, the letters <u>y</u> and <u>w</u> sometimes represent _____ sounds.

i    o
u
vowel

2. Letter-sound relationships for vowels closely follow the categories used for _____ . Thus, there are single vowels as well as vowel clusters.

consonants

## SINGLE VOWELS

| | |
|---|---|
| **3.** Single vowels include long vowels, short vowels, <u>r</u>-controlled vowels, and <u>y</u> when it functions as a single _____ . | vowel |
| **4.** A long vowel sound is identical to the vowel names of the traditional vowel letters: <u>a</u>, <u>e</u>, <u>i</u>, <u>o</u>, and <u>u</u>. Thus, the vowel in the word *mine* represents the _____ , or glided, vowel sound for <u>i</u>. In the word *make*, you hear a long, or glided, _____ sound. | long<br><br>a |
| **5.** Long vowel sounds occur most frequently in two positions: (1) when a vowel occurs at the _____ of a word or syllable such as *me*, *no*, *pa*-per, *ce*-dar, and *ci*-der, and (2) when a vowel is followed by a consonant and the letter <u>e</u> at the end of a _____ , such as *mane*, *time*, *rope*, and *cute*. The final <u>e</u> in this pattern is usually _____ . | end<br><br><br><br>word<br>silent (or a marker) |
| **6.** Each of the five traditional vowel letters also represents a short, or unglided, vowel sound. These _____ vowel sounds are often learned along with a set of key words:<br>  <u>a</u> as in *apple*<br>  <u>e</u> as in *egg*<br>  <u>i</u> as in *ink*<br>  <u>o</u> as in *octopus*<br>  <u>u</u> as in *umbrella* | short |
| **7.** Short _____ sounds occur most frequently in a word or syllable that ends in a consonant or consonant cluster such as *hap*-py, *let*, *win*, *ot*-ter, or *fun*. | vowel |
| **8.** Now look at this set of key words for both long and short vowels. Key words for vowel sound identification:<br>  *Apple* is the key word for the _____ sound of _____ .<br>  *Apron* is the key word for the _____ sound of _____ . | short<br>a<br>long<br>a |

| | |
|---|---|
| *Egg* is the key word for the _____ sound of _____ . | short    e |
| *Eleven* is the key word for the _____ sound of | long |
| _____ . | e |
| *Ink* is the key word for the _____ sound of _____ . | short    i |
| *Ice* is the key word for the _____ sound of _____ . | long    i |
| *Octopus* is the key word for the _____ sound of | short |
| _____ . | o |
| *Oat* is the key word for the _____ sound of _____ . | long    o |
| *Umbrella* is the key word for the _____ sound of | short |
| _____ . | u |
| *Use* is the key word for the _____ sound of _____ . | long    u |

**9.** When a vowel is followed by <u>r</u>, the <u>r</u> influences the vowel sound. These sounds are called _____ -controlled vowel sounds. They are neither long nor short but have a sound determined largely by the following <u>r</u>.

r

Key words for the identification of <u>r</u>-controlled vowel sounds follow:

*Car* is the key word for the vowel sound of _____ .    ar

*Her* is the key word for the vowel sound of _____ .    er

*Bird* is the key word for the vowel sound of _____ .    ir

*For* is the key word for the vowel sound of _____ .    or

*Turn* is the key word for the vowel sound of _____ .    ur

Note that three of these sounds will be identical in many dialects. Which graphemes are often used to designate the same phoneme? _____ , _____ , and _____ .    er   ir   ur

**10.** The letter <u>y</u> may function as a single consonant or a single vowel. <u>Y</u> functions as a vowel when it appears in two positions. First, <u>y</u> functions as a vowel when it appears at the end of a word with more than _____ syllable as in *sandy, baby,* or *sixty.* In this case, <u>y</u> often represents the _____ /ee/ sound.

one

long

Second, <u>y</u> functions as a vowel when it appears at the end of a word with only one syllable. In this case, <u>y</u> usually represents the long _____ sound as in words like *try, my,* or *cry.*

i

**11.** For the following list of words, identify the vowel sounds.

| | | |
|---|---|---|
| ape | _____ | long a |
| far | _____ | r-controlled a |
| we | _____ | long e |
| nice | _____ | long i |
| sly | _____ | long i |
| fir | _____ | r-controlled i |
| sticky | _____ _____ | short i    long e |
| fan | _____ | short a |
| mute | _____ | long u |
| met | _____ | short e |
| try | _____ | long i |
| tin | _____ | short i |
| on | _____ | short o |

# VOWEL CLUSTERS

## Digraphs

**12.** Like consonants, vowels also appear in clusters. Vowel
_____ consist of two or three vowel letters that often
appear together, such as <u>ou</u>, <u>ee</u>, <u>ai</u>, and <u>oy</u>. There are two types of
vowel clusters: vowel digraphs and vowel blends.

clusters

**13.** <u>Two vowels appearing together that represent a single</u>
<u>_____ are called vowel _____</u> .

phoneme    digraphs

**14.** The following key words are examples of the most common
vowel _____ .

*Meet* is the key word for the vowel _____ _____ .

*Ceiling* is the key word for the _____ digraph

_____ .

*Toe* is the key word for the vowel _____ _____ .

*Pie* is the key word for the vowel digraph _____ .

*Easy* is the key word for the vowel digraph _____ .

*Rain* is the key word for the vowel digraph _____ .

*Boat* is the key word for the _____ digraph _____ .

*Play* is the key word for the vowel digraph _____ .

*Grow* is the key word for the vowel digraph _____ .

digraphs

digraph    ee

vowel

ei

digraph    oe

ie

ea

ai

vowel    oa

ay

ow

| | |
|---|---|
| Pronounce each key word. Note that the above vowel _____ all result in a (long or short) _____ vowel sound. These, then, can be called _____ vowel _____ . | digraphs<br>long<br>long          digraphs |

## 📖📖 Blends (Diphthongs)

| | |
|---|---|
| **15.** Vowel blends are a second type of vowel cluster. <u>Vowel blends are two vowel letters that appear together and represent a blending of the sounds often associated with each letter like <u>oi</u> (soil), <u>oy</u> (toy), or <u>ou</u> (mouse)</u>. In each letter, you can hear elements of each vowel _____ blended together. Some people refer to vowel blends by another name, *diphthongs*. | sound |

| | |
|---|---|
| **16.** Here are the key words for vowel blends or _____ :<br>*Oil* is the key word for the diphthong _____ .<br>*Boy* is the key word for the diphthong _____ .<br>*Cow* is the key word for the diphthong _____ .<br>*Out* is the key word for the diphthong _____ .<br><br>Note that each of these four diphthongs represent _____ phonemes. | diphthongs<br>oi<br>oy<br>ow<br>ou<br><br>two |

| | |
|---|---|
| **17.** Oil and boy contain the same _____ sound.<br>Cow and out contain the same vowel sound.<br><br>Therefore, <u>oy</u> and _____ represent the same vowel _____ , and <u>ou</u> and _____ represent the same _____ sound. | vowel<br><br><br>oi<br>sound          ow<br>vowel |

| | | |
|---|---|---|
| **18.** Let's summarize. <u>Digraphs and diphthongs are two types of _____ clusters. Each is composed of _____ vowels.</u><br><u>A digraph represents _____ sound. A diphthong represents a blend of _____ vowel sounds within a single syllable.</u><br>Indicate if the following words contain digraphs or diphthongs: | vowel          two<br>one<br>two | |
| *pout*   _____ | diphthong | |
| *toy*   _____ | diphthong | |
| *snow*   _____ | digraph | |
| *clout*   _____ | diphthong | |
| *coat*   _____ | digraph | |
| *read*   _____ | digraph | |
| *how*   _____ | diphthong | |

## VOWEL GENERALIZATIONS

**19.** Letter-sound relationships for vowels are often determined by their locations within words and syllables. These locations are often labeled by the pattern of consonants (c) and vowels (v) that exist. Thus, a <u>cvc</u> pattern represents a vowel that appears in a word or syllable surrounded by two _____ such as the word *hot*. A <u>cv</u> pattern represents a word or syllable in which the vowel appears at the _____ of a word or syllable such as the word *me*. The following generalizations, like most other phonic rules, do not apply all the time. Nevertheless, familiarity with these patterns may often assist children who are unable to recognize an unfamiliar word.

consonants

end

### Vowel Generalization Number 1 (cvc or vc)

**20.** Look at the following single-syllable words:

*get*     *bag*     *fun*     *rid*     *hot*     *at*     *is*

In each of the words above, there is _____ vowel. The final letter in each word is a _____ .

one

consonant

The <u>e</u> in *get* sounds like the <u>e</u> in (egg or eve) _____ .

egg

The <u>e</u> represents the _____ <u>e</u> phoneme.

short

The <u>a</u> in *bag* sounds like the <u>a</u> in (an or ate) _____ .

an

The <u>a</u> represents the _____ <u>a</u> phoneme.

short

The <u>u</u> in *gum* represents the _____ <u>u</u> phoneme.

short

The <u>i</u> in *rid* has a _____ sound.

short

The <u>o</u> in *hot* has a _____ sound.

short

The <u>i</u> in *is* has a _____ sound.

short

**21.** Complete the following generalization:

In single-syllable words, when there is _____ vowel in a word and the word ends in a _____ , the vowel usually represents the _____ sound.

one

consonant

short

Another way of stating this generalization is:

The vowel is usually _____ when a single-syllable word ends in a _____ .

short

consonant

### 📖 Vowel Generalization Number 2 (cv)

22. Look at the following words:

| *go* | *he* | *hi* | *me* | |
|---|---|---|---|---|

In each of the above words, there is _____ vowel. That | one

vowel is at the _____ of the word. | end

The o in *go* sounds like the *o* in (open or on) _____ . | open

The o in *go* has a _____ sound. | long

The e in *he* sounds like the *e* in (egg or eve) _____ . | eve

The i in *hi* has a _____ sound. | long

The e in *me* has a _____ sound. | long

---

23. Complete the following generalization:

When the only vowel in a word is at the _____ of the | end

word, the vowel is usually _____ . | long

---

24. Another way of stating this generalization is:

The vowel sound is usually _____ when the vowel is the | long

_____ letter in the word. | final

---

### 📖 Vowel Generalization Number 3 (vce)

25. Look at the following words:

| *ride* | *rope* | *make* | *use* | |
|---|---|---|---|---|

There are _____ vowels in each word. The last letter in | two

each word is _____ . The final e is separated from the first | e

vowel by _____ consonant. | one

The i in *ride* sounds like the *i* in (it or ice) _____ . | ice

The o in *rope* sounds like the *o* in (open or on) _____ . | open

The a in *make* has a (long or short) _____ sound. | long

The first vowel in *use* has a _____ sound. | long

The final e in *ride, rope, make,* and *use* is _____ . The | silent

final e can be considered a marker for this spelling pattern.

---

26. Complete the following generalization:

When a word has two vowels, one of which is a final

_____ , separated from the first vowel by one consonant, | e

the first vowel usually has a _____ sound and the e is | long

usually _____ . | silent (or a marker)

| | |
|---|---|
| **27.** Another way of stating this generalization is: | |
| The final <u>e</u> is usually _____ , indicating that the preceding | silent (or a marker) |
| vowel has a _____ sound in words where the final <u>e</u> and | long |
| preceding vowel are separated by _____ consonant. | one |

### Vowel Generalization Number 4 (vv)

| | | |
|---|---|---|
| **28.** Look at the following words: | | |
| *rain     eat     boat     play     meet* | | |
| In the above words, there are _____ vowels. The pattern | two | |
| of two consecutive vowels gives a clue to the expected vowel | | |
| sound. | | |
| Pronounce the word *rain*. You hear the _____ | long | |
| _____ sound. The <u>i</u> is _____ . The second vowel is | a | silent |
| a marker for this spelling pattern. | | |
| Pronounce the word <u>eat</u>. You hear the _____ | long | |
| _____ sound. The <u>a</u> is _____ . | e | silent (or a marker) |
| *Boat* has a _____ <u>o</u> and a _____ <u>a</u>, | long | silent (or a marker) |
| *Play* has a _____ <u>a</u> and a _____ <u>y</u>, | long | silent (or a marker) |
| *Meet* has a _____ <u>e</u> and a _____ <u>e</u>. | long | silent (or a marker) |

| | | |
|---|---|---|
| **29.** Common double vowel combinations that usually result in a long | | |
| sound are <u>ai</u>, _____ , <u>oa</u>, <u>ay</u>, _____ . | ea | ee |

| | |
|---|---|
| **30.** Complete the following generalization: | |
| <u>When there are two consecutive vowels in a word, the first one</u> | |
| <u>usually has a _____ sound and the second one is usually</u> | long |
| <u>_____ unless they are vowel diphthongs.</u> | silent (or a marker) |

| | |
|---|---|
| **31.** Another way of stating this generalization is: | |
| A _____ vowel sound is usually produced when two | long |
| vowels appear side by side. The vowel sound heard is the long | |
| _____ of the first vowel; the second vowel is | sound |
| _____ (or a marker) unless the two vowels are vowel | silent |
| _____ . | diphthongs |

# SELF-CHECK FOR CHAPTER FOUR

| | |
|---|---|
| 1. You have noticed that a vowel may have a long _____ in three contexts.<br>First, a word that ends in <u>e</u> preceded by a _____ consonant usually has a _____ sound for the first vowel. Second, when there are two consecutive vowels, the _____ vowel is usually long and the second one is silent (or a marker) unless the two vowels are a _____ . Third, when the only vowel comes at the _____ of a syllable or word, that vowel is usually long. | sound<br><br>single<br><br>long<br><br>first<br>diphthong<br>end |
| 2. Short vowel sounds end in a syllable or word that ends in a _____ or consonant cluster. | consonant |
| 3. <u>R</u>-controlled vowels are neither long nor _____ . They have a sound determined by the following _____ . | short<br>r |
| 4. <u>Y</u> represents the long _____ sound when it appears at the end of a word with more than two syllables. <u>Y</u> has the long _____ sound when it appears at the end of a word with only one syllable. | e<br><br>i |
| 5. There are two types of vowel clusters: vowel _____ and vowel _____ or diphthongs. | digraphs<br>blends |
| 6. A digraph represents _____ sound. A _____ represents a blend of two vowel sounds. | one    blend (diphthong) |
| 7. A vowel usually represents the _____ sound when a single-syllable word ends in a _____ . | short<br>consonant |
| 8. When the only vowel in a word appears at the end, the vowel is usually _____ . | long |
| 9. When a word has two vowels, one of which is a final <u>e</u>, separated from the first vowel by one consonant, the first vowel usually represents the _____ sound and the _____ is usually silent. | long    e |

10. A _____ vowel sound is usually produced when two vowels appear side by side. The first vowel represents the _____ sound, whereas the second is usually _____ .

long

long    silent (or a marker)

# Context

Readers use many strategies to identify and pronounce words that might be unfamiliar to them in print. Often, such words are in a reader's speaking or listening vocabularies. Readers often use context clues to identify and pronounce these words. Context clues include the use of surrounding information to help you identify a word. They are very important aids to word analysis and comprehension.

Often, we forget that context operates at many levels to help readers determine pronunciation. Usually, context clues refer to the text surrounding an unfamiliar word and are thought of as syntactic (or language structure) clues, along with meaning (or semantic) clues. For example, in the sentence, *John went to the _____* , the language structure provides a clue for the type of word (the part of speech) that is appropriate for the blank—in this case, a noun. But it does not indicate the exact word that belongs in the blank. If the reader noticed and pronounced the first letters of the last word as <u>st</u> (e.g., *John went to the st_____* .), then the reader might predict that the target word was *store* or *street* and would use the sentences that followed the word to confirm or reject that prediction.

Similarly, if the reader noticed that the first letter began with <u>c</u>, a prediction might be deferred until looking at the sentence following the target word. If the two sentences were, *John went to the c_____* and *He paid for three pairs of socks*, the second sentence helps the reader to infer that the target word is probably *cashier*. Prediction of meaning, as well as pronunciation, is a significant element in using context clues. In addition to surrounding print, however, other context clues, such as pictures, provide help with meaning and pronunciation.

Context does not only apply to a whole word; it applies to within word context as well as to discourse-level context. For example, a reader can use knowledge of letter patterns to provide supportive contexts within words (what is the letter that follows q in English?). A reader can also use discourse knowledge as a form of context to provide predicted endings to familiar story structures (you can probably predict the end of a story that begins, *Once upon a time*) and to help pronounce words that appear often in specific story structures (e.g., *The pr_____* in a fairy tale is more likely to be *The prince* than *The primate*).

In all cases, a reader's background knowledge interacts greatly with context clues to aid a reader with unfamiliar words in print. Notice that one's knowledge about where one pays for socks helps a reader to determine that *cashier* would be the word in our first example. Similarly, a picture of a person walking toward a cash register station, one's familiarity with what letter follows a q in English, and what words are likely to appear in fairy tales work together with one's background knowledge to help determine pronunciation and meaning when reading.

For children in the early elementary grades, unfamiliar words encountered in their reading materials are usually part of their listening and speaking vocabularies. Thus, using meaningful context is often the most helpful word analysis strategy. Syntactic (or language patterning) clues and the semantic (or meaning) clues function together with a reader's linguistic and experiential background knowledge. Readers integrate the clues from all of these systems of language in the reading process.

## THE IMPORTANCE AND USE OF CONTEXT

| | | |
|---|---|---|
| **1.** | Readers use a variety of strategies to help them pronounce an unfamiliar word. One of the most important strategies is the use of _____ clues. | context |
| **2.** | When trying to determine the pronunciation and _____ of an unfamiliar word, readers can use several types of context clues. | meaning |

| | |
|---|---|
| **3.** Perhaps the most commonly used context is the information surrounding an unfamiliar word. In addition, readers use their linguistic and _____ knowledge to help them with unfamiliar words. Pictures and knowledge of story _____ are also important sources of context clues. | background<br><br>structure (or grammar) |
| **4.** Each time readers encounter an unfamiliar word they apply one or more word analysis strategies, such as phonics, sight words, structural and morphemic analysis, use of the dictionary, and _____ to determine meaning and _____ . | context    pronunciation |
| **5.** Even when readers use strategies other than context, they often use _____ to check their efforts at pronunciation and to see if the word makes _____ . | context<br>sense |

## USING CONTEXT TO CHECK WORD ANALYSIS

| | |
|---|---|
| **6.** Readers use context to determine whether their word analysis techniques were successful. For example, say the following word to yourself:<br><br>*object*<br><br>In which of the following sentences does the word that you said best fit?<br>(a) I _____ to your insults.<br>(b) The _____ of the game is to win.<br>If your pronunciation was *ob'ject*, you had to pick sentence number _____ . If your pronunciation was *ob ject'*, you had to pick sentence number _____ . Neither pronunciation was right or wrong until checked within the _____ of the sentence. | <br><br><br><br><br><br><br><br><br><br>6(b)<br>6(a)<br><br>context |
| **7.** For another example, let's imagine that you looked at the word *hoping* and pronounced it /hop/-ing.<br>Would that be correct? (yes or no) _____ The word should be pronounced _____ -ing. | no<br>/hope/ |

| | |
|---|---|
| But, if you did not correctly recognize the pronunciation of the word and you checked the _____ from which the word came, you would probably be able to correct yourself.<br><br>(a) Mary was *hoping* for a nice birthday present. | context |
| **8.** In item 6, the use of context to check other word analysis efforts related to _____ and accent. In item 7, the morphemic composition influenced the meaning and the vowel _____ . | meaning<br><br>pronunciation |

## USING CONTEXT WITH OTHER WORD ANALYSIS TECHNIQUES

| | |
|---|---|
| **9.** Context is used in combination with other word analysis strategies. Sometimes, vowel pronunciation generalizations can be used to predict pronunciation, but _____ must be used to confirm such pronunciations. At other times, context might predispose a reader toward a certain pronunciation, but pronunciation generalizations force a _____ in the prediction. | context<br><br>change |
| **10.** Read the following sentence:<br>(a) I'm looking for some heavy metal. Please *lead* me to the *lead*.<br>In the example, a vowel pronunciation generalization predicts that each of the words written as *lead* is pronounced _____ . However, context as a word analysis strategy indicates that the first instance of *lead* needs to be a verb, and the second instance needs to be a noun. A reader's linguistic knowledge _____ with context and with the vowel pronunciation generalization to confirm the pronunciation /leed/ in the first instance and _____ in the second. | /leed/<br><br>interacts<br><br>/led/ |
| **11.** In the following sentence, context predicts a _____ , and if unaware of the initial p, most readers predict the word *brother*.<br>(a) Sarah, who was now six, had always wanted either a sister or a p_____ .<br>In this case, letter name knowledge overrides context clues and the reader goes on to read *pet*, which is a noun and thus confirmed by _____ . | noun<br><br>context |

**12.** At times, however, context does not help either to confirm or suggest the _____ of a word, even though it indicates the part of speech. For example, read the following:

(a) I always wanted a _____ and now I finally have one! My long wait for a _____ was over, and I am so happy! No longer would I be left out of the group.

Even though context _____ a noun, there are so many possibilities that context is not helpful in example 12(a).

> meaning

> predicts

**13.** Look also at the following example.

(a) I was told the *ethmoid* was broken. However, although it was painful, it was not life threatening.

Similarly, this example shows that unless an unfamiliar word is already in the reader's _____ vocabulary, attempts at pronunciation might be correct but will not result in _____ .

(Did you already know that *ethmoid* is a bone in your nose?)

> oral (speaking)
> meaning

## USING CONTEXT AS A BASIC WORD ANALYSIS TECHNIQUE TO DETERMINE MEANING

**14.** Many authors intentionally provide context _____ for their readers. Special efforts are often made when new or difficult _____ are introduced. The following examples illustrate several of the more commonly used techniques.

> clues

> words (terms)

**15.** *Example 1:* Jim and Joan played a *set* of tennis. A set of tennis is completed when one player has won six or more games by a margin of two games.

In this example, the author has provided a _____ for the term _____ of tennis.

If you were unfamiliar with tennis terminology, you could read this sentence with meaning because the author gave you a context _____ . The technique of defining words is usually limited to situations where the word is used for the first time in a passage.

> definition
> set

> clue

16. *Example 2:* Many young children are *hyperopic*, or farsighted. In this case, the author has provided a synonym for the _____ term. A *hyperopic* child is one who is _____ .

_____ are used in the same manner as definitions when the author wants to explain a difficult word or concept.

unfamiliar

farsighted

Synonyms

17. *Example 3:* Suburban dwellers watch with amazement as their residential areas grow more and more crowded. They are witnessing, in many cases, the development of a *megalopolis*. High-rise apartments, shopping centers, new housing developments, schools, and recreation areas spring into being almost overnight. For example, the area between Baltimore, MD, and Washington, DC, is growing at such a rate that it will soon be one continuous area of dwellings and businesses.

In the above paragraph, readers can tell that *megalopolis* is the continuous development of _____ areas.

metropolitan

Readers can use two clues. Their first clue is that the topic being discussed is related to suburban development. Their second clue is an _____ .

example

18. *Example 4:* Many children came to Mary's birthday party. They played games, ate cake and ice cream, and sang "Happy Birthday" to Mary. It was one of the best days of Mary's life. She was *ecstatic*. In Example 4, the mood of the story was the _____ to the meaning of *ecstatic*. *Ecstatic*, as used in the above context, means very _____ . Readers might not know how to pronounce the word *ecstatic*, but they can come closer to an accurate meaning due to the _____ created by the story.

clue

happy

mood

19. *Example 5:* Reading aloud can cause anguish for some children. John, a boy of ten, suffered much embarrassment because he was shy and felt that he read badly aloud. He felt terrible, almost tortured, when asked to read aloud.

In Example 5, the _____ are provided for the term *anguish* by an example. In such cases, the author attempts to relate to an experience that the reader can understand. Many authors find that the use of _____ makes their writing more meaningful.

clues

examples

| | |
|---|---|
| **20.** Authors find many ways to help readers discover the meaning of words by providing _____ clues. The examples given above provide a few of the common types of context clues. Definition, example, _____ , and _____ are common types of context clues. Other important things that readers know in order to use context effectively appear below. | context<br><br>synonym    mood<br><br>同義字. |
| **21.** In order to use context effectively, readers need to be flexible in using surrounding text. In the following example, the context clues are provided _____ the target word.<br>(a) The teenager had been swimming since she was an infant. It is not surprising that she is a really good *swimmer*. | before |
| **22.** Read the following sentence:<br>(a) A *swimmer* is a person who swims.<br>In this example, the context clues are provided _____ the target word. | after |
| **23.** Context clues can also be provided by a _____ or apposi-tive phrase that follows the target word, as in<br>(a) He was *delayed*, or made late, because his car broke down.<br>(b) The *jockey* (a person who rides race horses) was very good at her job. | clause |
| **24.** Readers also use comparison patterns in using context to deter-mine meaning and pronunciation. _____ patterns can also require that readers read _____ the target word or look back at what preceded it.<br>(a) The *ancient* rock formations were as old as the earth itself.<br>(b) I hate going to bed early. In fact, I *despise* it. | Comparison<br>past (beyond) |
| **25.** Read the following sentences and decide how context can help to determine the italicized target word.<br>(a) My car is *quiet*, unlike the noisy thing that my brother drives!<br>(b) Even though I was fond of Bill, I truly *loved* Bob.<br>(c) It is *warm* during our winters, especially when compared to winter in Alaska.<br>The above sentences illustrate _____ patterns that help readers to use context clues. | contrast |

| | |
|---|---|
| **26.** Another pattern that helps readers to use context clues relies heavily on a reader's _____ knowledge. The following sentences illustrate an _____ pattern:<br>(a) Europe, Asia, North America, South America, Africa, Australia, and Antarctica are the seven *continents*.<br>(b) There are many high *mountains* in the world, but Mount Everest is the highest. | background<br><br>example |
| **27.** Although very useful, without appropriate background knowledge, an _____ pattern will not provide the context clues that are necessary to determine the target word. | example |

## LIMITATIONS OF THE USE OF CONTEXT CLUES

| | |
|---|---|
| **28.** From the above examples, you probably noticed that context clues have more to do with meaning than with _____ . It is possible that readers could use a synonym for an unfamiliar word when using _____ clues as their only form of word analysis. Other types of word _____ strategies, in combination with context clues, add to accuracy. | pronunciation<br><br><br>context<br><br>analysis |
| **29.** *Example:* Mary had a birthday _____ .<br>If the blank indicates an unfamiliar word, one might substitute words such as *today*, *surprise*, or_____ . However, because readers look closely at the initial consonant, when the example reads<br>(a) Mary had a birthday *p*_____ .<br>the reader's choices are limited. Now, of the words listed, only _____ will fit. | party (or other appropriate noun)<br><br><br><br><br><br><br>party |
| **30.** Readers might be able to supply a missing word in a sentence, but they might have a limited understanding of the word's _____ because they lack knowledge of the concept(s) that the word represents. | meaning |
| **31.** The use of context _____ should not be considered as a substitute for a complete program of vocabulary development. The more extensive readers' speaking and _____ vocabularies are, the greater their resources are for using context clues. | clues<br><br>listening |

| | |
|---|---|
| **32.** Another limitation of the use of context clues is that authors do not always supply the needed clue. Therefore, if readers rely only on the use of _____ , their word analysis strategies will not be as _____ as they could be. | context<br>effective |
| **33.** However, context clues are extremely helpful. As readers gain more experience with reading, and as their vocabulary and conceptual knowledge increase, they are _____ likely to use context. | more |
| **34.** Readers will find that they need to know the words and ideas _____ an unfamiliar word in order to use context effectively and that authors provide many different _____ of context clues. | around (surrounding)<br>types |
| **35.** Readers will also find the use of _____ to be an effective means for checking other attempts at _____ analysis. | context<br>word |

✔ **SELF-CHECK FOR CHAPTER FIVE**

| | |
|---|---|
| **1.** The following sentences contain language structure clues:<br>(a) John _____ to the store.<br>(b) The _____ is getting cold.<br>In sentence 1(a), you know the word will be a _____ . In sentence 1(b), you know the word will be a _____ . | verb<br>noun |
| **2.** Context clues can be used in the following ways:<br>(a) as a technique to determine the _____ of an unfamiliar word;<br>(b) to check a pronounced word to see if the word makes _____ ;<br>(c) as a step when using other _____ analysis strategies. | meaning<br><br>sense<br>word |
| **3.** The types of patterns that readers find useful when applying context clues are _____ patterns, _____ patterns, and _____ patterns. | comparison contrast<br>example |

# Sight Words

While all readers use a combination of the word analysis strategies discussed in this book, many words are recognized effortlessly and automatically. Such words are called *sight words* because they appear to be recognized and pronounced at sight, without conscious application of decoding or word analysis strategies. Mature readers recognize most words that they encounter in print by relying on their sight word knowledge. They develop this ability over time through extensive reading experiences. Beginning readers also recognize some words automatically, but they usually know relatively few words at sight. Beginning readers will develop their sight word knowledge by exposure to words in print and through extensive reading experiences. Through interaction with books and the words in those books, children will build sight word knowledge and a love of reading.

## THE DEVELOPMENT OF SIGHT WORD KNOWLEDGE

| | |
|---|---|
| 1. Words that do not require the conscious use of word _____ strategies are called sight words. These words are recognized and pronounced automatically, seemingly at _____ . | analysis<br><br>sight |
| 2. For mature readers, most of the words that they encounter are sight words but beginning readers also usually have some sight word _____ . | knowledge |

| | |
|---|---|
| **3.** Common sight words for _____ readers often include their name and "environmental print" that children often encounter throughout their day and talk about with adults. These words have become sight words because they have _____ for the child and have been seen _____ . | beginning<br><br><br><br>meaning<br>often |
| **4.** Sight words are recognized by a reader as a _____ unit, without the use of word analysis strategies. | whole |
| **5.** Sight words help a reader because a fairly small set of words appears _____ in writing. In fact, 200 words account for about 50 percent of the words in nearly _____ reading selection, and 400 words make up about 70 percent of most writing. | frequently (or often)<br>any |
| **6.** The ability to recognize and pronounce up to 70 _____ of reading selections at sight allows a reader to apply other word analysis strategies only when _____ . | percent<br><br>needed |
| **7.** Because 400 words make up about _____ percent of reading selections, these words are called high-frequency words. | 70 |
| **8.** Readers acquire most _____ -frequency words over time because they see these words so often. | high |
| **9.** At first, however, beginning readers try to recognize and pronounce these words by using other word analysis strategies, such as _____ or a phonic strategy. | context |
| **10.** Then, after repeated experiences with such words in meaningful context, these words become _____ words. | sight |
| **11.** Several people have provided lists of high-frequency words that appear in children's _____ materials. These lists can be helpful when teaching sight words to beginning _____ . | reading<br>readers |
| **12.** Perhaps the most well-known list is the Dolch List of Basic Sight Words. The _____ list, shown in Figure 1, contains 220 basic sight words. Recent analyses indicate that the Dolch list still accounts for about 50 percent of _____ in common K-3 reading material. | Dolch<br><br>words |

**Figure 1    Dolch List of Basic Sight Words**

| | | | | | |
|---|---|---|---|---|---|
| a | did | have | me | said | try |
| | do | he | much | saw | two |
| about | does | help | must | say | |
| after | done | her | my | see | |
| again | don't | here | myself | seven | under |
| all | down | him | | shall | up |
| always | draw | his | never | she | upon |
| am | drink | hold | new | show | us |
| an | | hot | no | sing | use |
| and | | how | not | sit | |
| any | eat | hurt | now | six | |
| are | eight | | | sleep | very |
| around | every | | of | small | |
| as | | I | off | so | walk |
| at | fall | if | old | some | want |
| | far | in | on | soon | warm |
| be | fast | into | once | start | was |
| because | find | is | one | stop | wash |
| been | first | it | only | | we |
| before | five | its | open | take | well |
| best | fly | | or | tell | went |
| bring | for | jump | our | ten | were |
| big | found | just | out | thank | what |
| black | four | | over | that | when |
| blue | from | keep | own | the | where |
| both | full | kind | | their | which |
| bring | funny | know | pick | them | white |
| brown | | | play | then | who |
| but | gave | laugh | please | there | why |
| buy | get | let | pretty | these | will |
| by | give | light | pull | they | wish |
| | go | like | put | think | with |
| call | goes | little | | this | work |
| came | going | live | ran | those | would |
| can | good | long | read | three | write |
| carry | got | look | red | to | |
| clean | green | | ride | today | yellow |
| cold | grow | made | right | together | yes |
| come | | make | round | too | you |
| could | had | many | run | | your |
| cut | has | may | | | |

---

| | |
|---|---|
| **13.** A more recent list has been compiled by Fry (1980), whose list of 300 New Instant Words is also highly regarded as representative of high- _____ words in written English. | frequency |
| **14.** Look at the words on the Dolch list in Figure 1. Why do you think this list has been so _____ , over decades, in representing high-frequency words? | stable (reliable) |

| | |
|---|---|
| **15.** Did you notice that many of the words appearing on the list are mainly function words; that is, they do not change much over _____ but are necessary to link content words? | time |
| **16.** Words such as *a, and, the, any, because,* and so on are used very _____ and their frequency of use has not changed through the years. It is not surprising, when looking carefully at a high-frequency word list, that these words account for so _____ of the words found in the text. | frequently (often) <br><br><br><br> many |
| **17.** Looking at the words on a high-frequency word list should also give you some insight into the kinds of words that should be _____ as sight words. | taught |
| **18.** Readers acquire most sight words _____ through reading experiences. However, it is appropriate to directly teach some useful sight words and to check children's development of sight word knowledge. | independently |
| **19.** The words that should be taught as initial sight words have three important characteristics. <br> First, words that should be _____ as initial sight words should appear frequently in print; they should be high-_____ words. Words like *the* as opposed to words like *monkey* should be taught as sight words. <br> Second, words that should be taught as initial sight words should have meanings that are in the reader's oral _____ . Words like *car* and *home* are more appropriate than words like *turbine*. <br> Third, words that should be taught as initial sight words often cannot be recognized or pronounced by applying phonic _____ . Teaching such words as sight words allows readers to recognize irregular words when they are encountered in print. Words like *one, said,* and *some* are examples of such words. | taught <br><br> frequency <br><br><br> vocabulary <br><br><br><br> generalizations |

| | |
|---|---|
| 20. Although sight word learning for beginning readers often involves words learned from high-frequency word lists and from their _____ , most words become sight words through readers' repeated _____ with words in print. | environment<br>interactions |
| 21. Thus, a good program of sight word instruction will emphasize wide _____ as well as provide initial, direct instruction of sight words for beginning readers. | reading |

## ✔ SELF-CHECK FOR CHAPTER SIX

| | |
|---|---|
| 1. When a word is recognized and pronounced automatically, it is called a _____ _____ . | sight word |
| 2. When teaching initial sight words to beginning readers, you should consider the following things when choosing the words to teach:<br>(a) the words should appear _____ in print;<br>(b) the words should be in the reader's _____ vocabulary;<br>(c) the words should not be pronounced using _____ generalizations. | frequently<br>oral<br>phonic |
| 3. Most sight words are learned _____ by readers through their own _____ experiences. | independently<br>reading |
| 4. It is important to provide meaningful reading experiences for beginning readers, partly because this helps to develop _____ _____ knowledge. | sight word |

# Developmental Spelling Patterns

Look at the following writers sample from a five year old:

   I LK MY KTY ("I like my kitty.")

Children tell us what they know about word analysis through the uncorrected spelling patterns that they use in their writing. From the sentence above, written by a five year old, we can learn many things. Because this child has written each word separately, we know that she has developed the ability to hear words as separate entities, an important aspect of phonological awareness. Because she has represented many of the phonemes as separate elements in her spelling, we also know that she has developed important aspects of phonemic awareness. Notice, too, the correct spelling of the high-frequency sight words "I" and "MY." This indicates that the child is developing sight word knowledge of these common words. We also know that the child has not yet developed an understanding of the vce pattern for long vowels since she spelled the word *like* as "LK." Finally, the child has not yet developed an understanding of the cvc pattern for short vowels since the word *kitty* is spelled "KTY." These last two clues may also tell us that the child may not as yet be able to identify vowel phonemes in the middle of a word, an important aspect of phonemic awareness.

   If you know what to look for, children's developmental spelling can be a powerful source of diagnostic information. It can indicate if children have developed phonemic awareness, which phonic patterns they understand, and which words they already know as sight words. Children's developmental spelling is a "window" to their word analysis knowledge, enabling you to see much of what they know and have as yet to learn about word analysis.

*Developmental spelling* refers to the spelling patterns children use during uncorrected writing. Children's developmental spelling progresses through a predictable series of phases until more standard spelling forms appear. If you understand the developmental progression of these phases, you can determine what children know and have as yet to learn about word analysis. Often, people use the term "invented" spelling instead of developmental spelling since children appear to invent the spelling rules through their writing activities, gradually inducing standard spelling patterns.

The developmental spelling checklist in Figure 1 will help you to analyze and track the progression of children's word analysis skills through the patterns of their uncorrected writing and spelling. It shows each of the five major phases of developmental spelling, patterns in each phase, and what the child knows about word analysis. This chapter will describe each of the major phases children pass through and explains how each phase indicates something important about their emerging skills with word analysis.

## Figure 1.   The Leu and Kinzer developmental spelling checklist. (Leu & Kinzer, 1999)

Student _____

Teacher _____

School Year _____

### A. Precommunicative Phase

School Quarter

| Pattern | What the child knows | I | II | III | IV |
|---|---|---|---|---|---|
| 1. Random drawing | Tool knowledge | | | | |
| 2. Organized lines | Left to right/There is a system here but what are the rules? | | | | |
| 3. Letter components | Letters are central elements | | | | |
| 4. Random letters | Letter formation | | | | |

### B. Semiphonetic Phase

School Quarter

| Pattern | What the child knows | I | II | III | IV |
|---|---|---|---|---|---|
| 1. Some systematic meaning | Letters represent sounds/sounds represent meaning | | | | |
| 2. Sounds of letters are names of letters | Letter names are letter sounds | | | | |
| 3. Consonants and long vowels, few short vowels | Consonants carry most information | | | | |
| 4. Spaces between words | What a written word is | | | | |

### C. Phonetic Phase

School Quarter

| Pattern | What the child knows | I | II | III | IV |
|---|---|---|---|---|---|
| 1. Most sounds represented in writing | Recognizes most phonological segments | | | | |
| 2. Phonic strategies are used | English is phonetic | | | | |

### D. Transitional Phase

School Quarter

| Pattern | What the child knows | I | II | III | IV |
|---|---|---|---|---|---|
| 1. Some irregular, high-frequency sight words spelled correctly | English is not phonetic | | | | |

### E. Standard Phase

School Quarter

| Pattern | What the child knows | I | II | III | IV |
|---|---|---|---|---|---|
| 1. Most words spelled correctly | English is and is not phonetic | | | | |
| 2. Misspellings follow these patterns: | | | | | |

_____

_____

_____

_____

**Developmental Spelling Patterns**     **67**

## THE PRECOMMUNICATIVE PHASE

**Figure 2.   An example of a child's writing from the precommunicative phase.**

1.  Children usually begin their writing in a precommunicative phase. (See Figure 2.) During this phase, writing is characterized by not having a consistent communicative intent. If you ask children what their writing says, they will not understand your question or will create a new _____ each time you ask. Their scribbles indicate that they are developing an understanding of the tools of writing: how to hold a pencil or crayon, how to use it to make marks, and so on.

    meaning

2.  Writing during the early precommunicative phase usually indicates that children have not yet developed phonological or phonemic awareness. We do not as yet see evidence of written words or letters representing _____ or sounds. Thus, it is likely that they may be unable to distinguish words, syllables, or sounds as separate units.

    words

3.  A little later in the precommunicative phase, organized lines of scribbles begin to emerge. Lines of scribble begin to flow from left to _____ , indicating that children have discovered this important principle in our writing system.

    right

4.  Still later, during the precommunicative phase, you may find common letter components appearing, such as circles, vertical lines, horizontal lines, and diagonal lines. Random letters will also appear but children will only be able to tell you the names of these letters, not what their message _____ . These features indicate that children are paying attention to letter forms in our writing system but have not as yet discovered the alphabetic _____ , or the insight that letters represent sounds.

    means

    principle

| | |
|---|---|
| 5. The precommunicative phase is an important one for children. It is a phase where they are forming the foundation for important steps, that is, the development of phonemic and phonological _____ and the discovery of the alphabetic _____ . | awareness    principle |

 **THE SEMIPHONETIC PHASE**

**Figure 3.** An example of a child's writing from the semiphonetic phase. ("I read the book.")

IRDB

| | |
|---|---|
| 6. Next, children usually enter a semiphonetic phase (see Figure 3). At this time, children discover that letters represent sounds in oral language. Developing an understanding of this _____ principle is an important step. It happens in conjunction with the development of phonological and _____ awareness. Both of these developments help children to discover that writing is used to communicate meaning. | alphabetic

phonemic |
| 7. During the semiphonetic _____ , children often believe that the names of the letters are the sounds they represent. Thus, messages like
    IM5 (I am five.)
may sometimes appear. | phase |
| 8. Most words are represented in written messages during the semi-phonetic phase. This suggests that children have developed _____ awareness since they can identify individual words. | phonological |

| | |
|---|---|
| **9.** Also, during this time, onset and final consonants appear much more frequently than medial _____ , as in these writing samples:<br><br>    I WT PZ DR (I want pizza for dinner.)<br>    SL T KN (The squirrel took the corn.)<br><br>This may suggest that the child is able to hear the initial and final phonemes in a word or syllable easier than a phoneme in the _____ of a word. | vowels<br><br><br><br><br><br><br><br>middle |
| **10.** Long vowel sounds are often represented in this phase, far more often than short vowels:<br><br>    KN U C BZ (Can you see the birds?)<br>    I LK BB SR (I like my baby sister.)<br><br>This may suggest that the child finds it easier to hear long vowel phonemes than short vowel _____ . It may also be due to the fact that letter names for vowels are identical to long vowel _____ . | phonemes<br><br>sounds |
| **11.** Often, children will begin to demonstrate knowledge of high-frequency sight words or words that are very important to them early in their writing. They demonstrate this by correctly spelling common _____ words such as *my, mom, me,* or *I:*<br><br>    ME N MOM R SK (Me and my mom were sick.)<br>    ILMICAT (I love my cat.) | sight |
| **12.** The _____ phase is an important milestone for children. It shows that they have developed an understanding of the _____ principle. Children in this phase understand that letters represent sounds, even though they are not able to hear successfully all of the sounds or represent each sound with a letter. This may suggest that children need to develop additional _____ awareness before moving into the next phase. | semiphonetic<br><br>alphabetic<br><br><br><br><br>phonemic |

### THE PHONETIC PHASE

| | |
|---|---|
| **13.** When you see writing that looks as if a child is trying to represent nearly every _____ in each word, it is likely that the child is in the _____ phase. | phoneme<br>phonetic |

**Figure 4.** An example of a child's writing from the phonetic phase. ("Frogs jumped.")

14. You will notice that more consonant and vowel sounds are beginning to be represented, although often in unconventional ways:

    I LIK TU GO SLEDIG (I like to go sledding.)

    ME N MI DOG WNT FRO A WLK (Me and my dog went for a walk.)

    This may indicate an increase in _____ awareness for children in this phase.

    phonemic

15. Children in the _____ phase believe that they have figured out the secret of writing: Words are always spelled the way they sound. Children in the phonetic phase believe that our spelling system is perfectly _____.

    phonetic

    alphabetic (regular)

**Figure 5.** An example of a child's writing from the transitional phase.

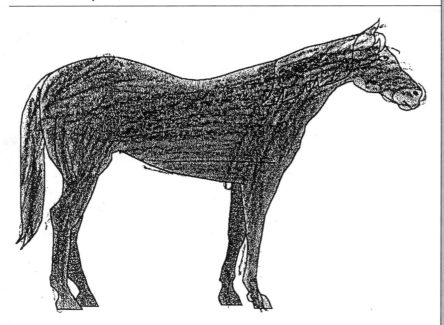

Brn hors brn hors wut do
You see I see a gra dog
tkn at me

16. During the transitional phase, you will see a number of irregular, high-frequency _____ words spelled correctly (see Figure 5). **sight**
    At the same time, other words will be spelled as if the child is still spelling them according to the way the words _____ . **sound**
    This is an important phase since it indicates that the child recognizes the fact that not all words are spelled as they sound.

**17.** During the transitional phase, writing often combines phonic strategies and sight word _____ . The sight words that appear are often very common words (e.g., *and, I, me*) or words that are very important to a child. Notice, for example, the sight words in these sentences:

> ME AND MY FRNDZ LIK TO PLA
>
> (Me and my friends like to play.)
>
> CAPPY MY DOG WZ HT BY A CAR
>
> (Cappy, my dog, was hit by a car.)

strategies

## THE STANDARD PHASE

**Figure 6.** An example of a child's writing from the standard phase.

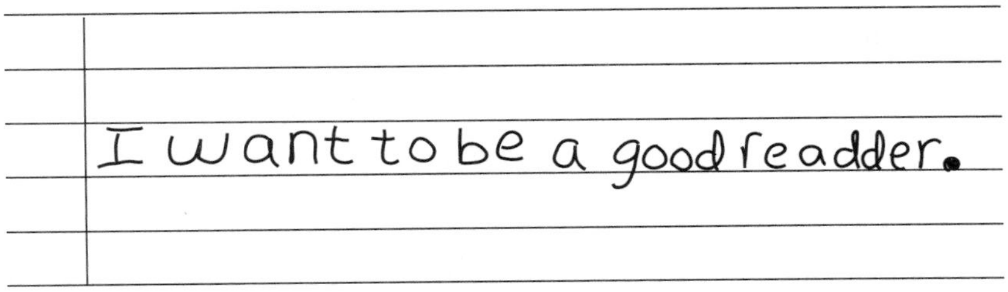

> I want to be a good reader.

**18.** During the _____ phase of developmental spelling, students are able to combine appropriately phonic and _____ word strategies (see Figure 6). For most of us, there will still be some words that are spelled incorrectly. These often are the same set of words or follow a particular pattern. The pattern might include, for example, the misspelling of words with single or double consonants or words that contain certain types of endings. This is another example:

> I liked reading this book because it was very *excitting* and it was about the pioneers.

standard

sight

**SELF-CHECK FOR CHAPTER SEVEN**

Look at this writing from a five year old:

    K P (The cat and the person)

| | |
|---|---|
| **1.** We can tell that this child has developed some elements of _____ awareness since each of the two words is represented as separate entities. | phonological |
| **2.** This child is probably in the _____ phase of developmental spelling. | semiphonetic |
| **3.** The child knows about the _____ progression of print. | left-to-right |
| **4.** We also know that this child is beginning to develop an understanding of the _____ principle since two initial consonant sounds are represented by letters. | alphabetic |
| **5.** This child has probably not as yet developed a complete sense of _____ awareness since not all of the phonemes are represented. | phonemic |
| Look at this writing from another five year old:<br><br>    OEPBEYET (I love my kitty.) | |
| **6.** We can tell that this child is in the _____ phase of developmental spelling since each time this child read the writing she generated a different message ("I love my kitty." "I played outside." "I went to school."). | precommunicative |
| **7.** We can also tell that the child understands how to form _____ and that writing progresses from left to right. | letters |
| **8.** This child has probably not as yet acquired an understanding of the _____ principle. | alphabetic |

Look at this writing from a six year old:

Me ND Jese DEAGO r fnz

(Me and Jesse Diego are friends.)

| | |
|---|---|
| 9. This child is probably in the _____ phase of developmental spelling since most sounds are represented phonetically. | phonetic |
| 10. We can also tell that this child has developed a good sense of phonemic _____ . | awareness |
| 11. This child will shortly learn that some words are spelled the way they sound but that some words are _____ . | not |

Look at this writing from another six year old:

I luv my Tarus that was a car adn I luv my mom adn my dad
adn we wtch TV.
(I love my Taurus, that was a car, and I love my mom and dad
and we watch TV.)

| | |
|---|---|
| 12. This child is probably in the _____ phase. Many words are spelled correctly although the sight word *and* is regularly misspelled. Several words are still being spelled the way this child _____ them rather than as sight words. | transitional<br><br>hears |
| 13. We can tell, however, that this child is beyond the phonetic phase and no longer believes that each word is _____ as it sounds. | spelled |
| 14. This child's understanding of phonemic awareness is fairly well developed since most _____ are represented in writing. | sounds |

# Morphemic and Structural Analysis

*Morphemic analysis* is the study of meaning units within words and includes structural analysis, which refers to dividing a word into its syllables. Because syllabication helps children to decode unfamiliar words, it is part of the decoding process. When looking at meaning units within words, we look at morphemes. A *morpheme* is the smallest unit of meaning in a word. Some morphemes can stand alone as a meaning-bearing unit. For example, the word *cat* contains a single morpheme and stands alone as a meaning-bearing unit. Such morphemes are called "free" morphemes. Other morphemes are meaning-bearing but cannot stand alone. For example, the s in *cats* has meaning, indicating that there is more than one cat. Yet the s cannot stand alone without *cat*. Morphemes such as the s in *cats* are called "bound" morphemes.

Morphemic analysis involves looking at word parts, such as prefixes, suffixes, and root words, to help determine a word's meaning. The content of morphemic analysis included in reading instruction is the study of *affixes* (i.e., both prefixes and suffixes), root words, and compound words. The study of word structure includes syllabication patterns as well as spelling patterns that are influenced by the addition of affixes.

## UNDERSTANDING AFFIXES

| | |
|---|---|
| **1.** "Affix" refers to a syllable or letter combination added to the beginning or _____ of a word to change its meaning or part of speech. An affix added to the beginning of a word is called a _____ . An affix added to the end of a word is called a _____ . Both prefixes and suffixes are called _____ . | end<br><br><br>prefix<br>suffix<br>affixes |

### Adding Prefixes

| | |
|---|---|
| **2.** Prefixes are added to the _____ of words to change their meaning. Add the prefix to the base (or root) words below:<br><br>un to the base *happy*      _____<br>dis to the base *regard*      _____<br>en to the base *able*      _____<br>ex to the base *change*      _____ | beginnings<br><br><br>unhappy<br>disregard<br>enable<br>exchange |
| **3.** Did you notice that the spelling of the root word was _____ changed when the prefix was added? | not |
| **4.** Was the meaning of the base word altered by the prefix? (yes or no) _____ | yes |

### Prefix Generalization

| | |
|---|---|
| **5.** When a prefix is added to a word, the spelling of the base word is usually not changed, but the _____ is changed.<br>Another way of stating this generalization is:<br>When added to a base word, a prefix changes the _____ but not the _____ of the base word. | meaning<br><br><br>meaning<br>spelling |
| **6.** Which of the following words fit this generalization?<br>*unknown   homeless   dislike   friendly   enlarge*<br><br>_____   _____   _____ | unknown   dislike   enlarge |

| | |
|---|---|
| 7. Read the following two sentences:<br><br>(a) John is *happy* to be in school.<br><br>(b) John is *unhappy* to be in school.<br><br>*Unhappy* differs from *happy* in that the _____ <u>un</u> is added to happy. | prefix |
| 8. You can tell the meaning of a prefix by noticing how it changes the meaning of the root word to which it is added. For example,<br><br>*happy* in sentence 7(a) means _____ .<br><br>*Unhappy* in sentence 7(b) means _____ glad.<br><br>Thus, the prefix <u>un</u> means _____ . | glad<br><br>not<br><br>not |
| 9. From the following list of words, identify the prefix and indicate the meaning of the prefix. | |

| | *Prefix* | *Meaning* | | |
|---|---|---|---|---|
| *dislike* | _____ | _____ | dis | not |
| *enable* | _____ | _____ | en | make |
| *inconsistent* | _____ | _____ | in | not |
| *unseen* | _____ | _____ | un | not |
| *retake* | _____ | _____ | re | again |
| *preview* | _____ | _____ | pre | before |

| | |
|---|---|
| The meaning of a _____ can be determined by the manner in which it _____ the meaning of the base word. | prefix<br>changes (alters) |

## 📖📖 Adding Suffixes

| | |
|---|---|
| 10. Suffixes are additions to the _____ of root words and can alter both a word's grammatical function (part of speech) and/or its meaning. There are two important types of suffix. One type of suffix is called an *inflectional ending* or inflection. Another type of suffix is a *derivational suffix*. | ends |

**11.** An inflectional ending often changes the grammatical function but not the core meaning of the root word to which it is added. Common _____ endings are <u>s</u>, <u>es(s)</u>, <u>ing</u>, <u>ed</u>, <u>er</u>, <u>est</u>, and <u>ly</u>.

Notice how the inflectional endings in the words below do not alter the root word's central meaning:

| | | | |
|---|---|---|---|
| cat | cat<u>s</u> | singular changed to _____ | plural |
| host | host<u>ess</u> | masculine changed to _____ | feminine |
| lean | lean<u>er</u> | adjective changed to _____ | comparative |
| happy | happi<u>ly</u> | adjective changed to _____ | adverb |

inflectional  朋 肥

**12.** Apostrophes followed by <u>s</u> also are categorized as inflectional _____ . For example, the meaning of *cat*, followed by <u>'s</u> changes to indicate _____ .

endings

possession

---

📖 **Suffix Generalization Number 1**

**13.** Add the inflectional ending <u>ing</u> to these words:

| | |
|---|---|
| *hope* | _____ |
| *love* | _____ |
| *write* | _____ |
| *make* | _____ |

hoping
loving
writing
making

**14.** To add the inflectional ending <u>ing</u>, the final <u>e</u> was _____ from the base word.

dropped (omitted)

**15.** Complete the following generalization:

When adding the inflectional ending _____ to a base word that ends in <u>e</u>, you usually drop the _____ and add the inflectional ending.

ing
vowel (e)

**16.** Which of the following words fit this pattern?

*stopping    filing    fusing    cunning    tubing*

_____    _____    _____

filing    fusing    tubing

| | |
|---|---|
| **17.** This generalization also applies to these words when inflectional endings that begin with a vowel are added. Apply this generalization by adding the suffix to the following words:<br><br>ed to *hop*e _____<br>er to *write* _____<br>es to *love* _____<br>ing to *make* _____ | hoped<br>writer<br>loves<br>making |
| **18.** Complete the following generalization:<br>When adding an inflectional ending that begins with a<br><br>_____ to a base word that ends in _____ , you usu-<br><br>ally drop the final _____ and add the inflectional ending. | vowel   e<br><br>e |

📖 **Suffix Generalization Number 2**

| | |
|---|---|
| **19.** Above the last three letters in the following words, mark <u>v</u> over the vowels and <u>c</u> over the consonants, as shown with *hop*.<br><br>cvc<br>——<br>*hop*        ——        ——        ——<br>            *occur*      *sit*      *skip*<br>What is the pattern that you notice? _____ | cvc   cvc   cvc<br>occur  sit   skip<br><br>cvc |
| **20.** Add <u>ing</u> to *hop* and *sit*.<br><br>_____   _____<br><br>Add <u>ed</u> to *occur* and *skip*.<br><br>_____   _____ | hopping    sitting<br><br><br>occurred    skipped |
| **21.** There are two important things to notice in the example shown in item 20. First, do the inflectional endings in item 22 begin with a vowel or consonant? _____<br>Second, in order to add the inflectional ending, the final consonant in the root word was _____ . | vowel<br><br><br>doubled |

| | |
|---|---|
| **22.** Based on what you noticed in item 20, complete the following generalization:<br><br>When adding an inflectional ending that begins with a vowel to a base word that has a _____ pattern for its last three letters, the last consonant of the root word usually should be _____ .<br><br>Another way of stating this generalization is:<br><br>The last consonant is _____ when you add an inflectional ending that begins with a _____ to a word that ends in the pattern _____ . | cvc<br><br><br>doubled<br><br><br>doubled<br>vowel<br>cvc |
| **23.** Which of the following words fit this pattern?<br>*rubbing    minded    shamed    batted    bidder*<br><br>_____    _____    _____ | rubbing    batted    bidder |

**Suffix Generalization Number 3**

| | |
|---|---|
| **24.** To determine Suffix Generalization Number 3, you will be asked to state what you notice in the following example:<br><br>Add:<br><br>ing to *sleep*          _____<br>ed to *wash*          _____<br>er to *short*          _____<br>en to *eat*          _____ | <br><br><br><br>sleeping<br>washed<br>shorter<br>eaten |
| **25.** Do the root words in item 24 end in a vowel or a consonant?<br><br>_____ | consonant |
| **26.** Do any of the base words in item 24 end in the pattern <u>cvc</u>? (yes or no) _____ | no |
| **27.** What do you notice about the inflectional endings in item 24?<br>These inflectional endings begin with a _____ | vowel |
| **28.** Is either the base word or the suffix changed when they are joined? (yes or no) _____ | no |

**29.** Based on your observations about the examples in item 24, complete the following generalization:

When you add an inflectional ending that begins with a vowel to a base word that ends in a consonant, but not in the pattern of _____ , neither the _____ nor the inflectional ending is changed when they are joined.

Another way of stating this generalization is:

Inflectional endings are added without changing the spelling of the base word when the base word ends with a _____ but not with the cvc _____ .

| | |
|---|---|
| cvc | base |
| consonant | |
| pattern | |

**30.** Which of the following words fit this pattern?

*baiting    bidding    willing    hurting    nicer    beaded*

_____    _____

_____    _____

| | |
|---|---|
| baiting | willing |
| hurting | beaded |

### Suffix Generalization Number 4

**31.** Note the pattern of the last two letters of the following words:

*try*                    *candy*
*cry*                    *fly*

The last letter in each word is _____ , which is preceded by a _____ .

y
consonant

**32.** Add the inflectional endings to the following words:

ed to *try*        _____

es to *candy*      _____

ed to *cry*        _____

es to *fly*        _____

| |
|---|
| tried |
| candies |
| cried |
| flies |

**33.** The last letter in each of the above base words was _____ , and was changed to _____ before the inflectional ending was added. The inflectional endings in item 32 begin with the letter _____ .

y    i

e

**34.** Complete the following generalization:

When you add an inflectional ending that begins with

_____ to a base word that ends in a consonant plus a

_____ pattern, you usually change the y to

_____ and add the inflectional ending.

Another way of stating this generalization is:

Change the y to _____ when you add an inflectional

ending beginning with a vowel to words ending with a

_____ plus a _____ .

| |
|---|
| e |
| y |
| i |
| i |
| consonant    y |

**35.** Which ones of the following words fit the above pattern:
*sizing    armies    busses    pennies    ladies*

_____    _____    _____

| |
|---|
| armies    pennies    ladies |

✔ ## SELF-CHECK FOR INFLECTED ENDINGS (SUFFIXES)

**1.** Add the inflected endings to the items below.

| | |
|---|---|
| ed to *bless* | _____ |
| ing to *drive* | _____ |
| er to *boast* | _____ |
| est to *lazy* | _____ |

| |
|---|
| blessed |
| driving |
| boaster |
| laziest |

**2.** If readers look at *sloping* and do not know it at sight, they might
try to take off the _____ and examine the root word.
After taking off the ing suffix, _____ would be left.

| |
|---|
| suffix (ing) |
| slop |

**3.** Note the structure of what is left after the ing suffix is removed. It
apparently ends in what type of letter pattern? _____

| |
|---|
| cvc |

**4.** Was the final consonant doubled when the ing was added? (yes or
no) _____

| |
|---|
| no |

**5.** Given that the final consonant was not doubled, would you say
that *slop* is the root word? (yes or no) _____

| |
|---|
| no |

**6.** *Slop* is not the root word because the final consonant was not
_____ when the suffix was added.

| |
|---|
| doubled |

**7.** The base word for *sloping* is, therefore, probably _____ .

| |
|---|
| slope |

| | |
|---|---|
| **8.** Note that this visual clue guides the reader to the pronunciation of the word since the final <u>e</u> determines the _____ of the first vowel. | sound |
| **9.** A reader would have to imagine the base word to be _____ with the inflectional ending _____ added. | slope<br>ing |
| **10.** Write the base word for the following words:<br><br>*sloping* _____<br>*temping* _____<br>*slopping* _____<br>*dozing* _____<br>*given* _____ | slope<br>temp<br>slop<br>doze<br>give |

## SYLLABICATION

| | |
|---|---|
| **1.** Recognizing syllable units within words is another word analysis strategy that falls under the heading of structural analysis. Syllables usually do not have _____ in themselves but, by breaking words into smaller parts, the reader is often able to pronounce the parts and blend them into familiar words. | meaning |
| **2.** Although some syllabication generalizations may be important for teachers and children to know, others are so inconsistent that they are of _____ value. We have placed the most consistent and useful syllable generalizations in this section. | little |
| **3.** Sometimes, criticism of syllabication as a word analysis technique occurs because of the manner in which it is taught. Syllables should be _____ as visual clues, not as sounding clues. For example, one cannot start with a statement such as, "If the vowel is long, divide the syllable after the vowel." In this instance, a generalization is not needed because the word has _____ been pronounced. | taught<br><br><br><br><br>already |

### Syllabication Generalization Number 1

| | |
|---|---|
| **4.** Would you guess that the number of syllables in a word is more closely related to the number of vowels or to the number of consonants in that word? _____ | vowels |

**5.** How many vowel sounds do you have in each word below?

| | | | | | |
|---|---|---|---|---|---|
| *cat* | _____ | *apple* | _____ | one | two |
| *happiness* | _____ | *rate* | _____ | three | one |
| *philosophy* | _____ | *tiger* | _____ | four | two |

Are there the same number of syllables as there are vowel

sounds? (yes or no) _____          yes

**6.** Complete the following generalization:

There are as many syllables in a word as there are vowel

_____ .          sounds (phonemes)

Another way of stating this generalization is:

The number of vowel _____ in a word is the same as the          sounds (phonemes)

number of _____ .          syllables

### 📖 Syllabication Generalization Number 2

**7.** How many vowel sounds do you hear in the following words:

| | | | | | |
|---|---|---|---|---|---|
| *hope* | _____ | *love* | _____ | one | one |
| *write* | _____ | *hate* | _____ | one | one |

Each of the above words has _____ vowels. The final          two

_____ is silent.          e

**8.** How many vowel sounds do you hear in the following words?

| | | | | | |
|---|---|---|---|---|---|
| *read* | _____ | *feed* | _____ | one | one |
| *rain* | _____ | *coat* | _____ | one | one |

How many vowels are in these words? _____ The second          two

_____ in these words is _____ (a pattern marker).          vowel     silent

**9.** Complete the following generalization:

There are two situations when a vowel letter usually does not

represent a sound. When these structures appear, there are

_____ vowels but only one vowel _____ ; thus,          two     sound

the two vowels are in one syllable.

**10.** These first two generalizations relate directly to the knowledge

that children should have prior to learning the remaining general-

izations. As such, they are not really generalizations applied to

_____ but refer, instead, to some visual and sound clues          syllabication

available in the language.

## Syllabication Generalization Number 3 (<u>vc/cv</u>)

**11.** Place a <u>v</u> over the first and last vowels in the words and a <u>c</u> over the consonants that are between the vowels, as shown below:

       <u>vccv</u>
*Example:* picnic

        *pencil*             *index*

        *window*

The words are all similar in that they contain the _____ pattern.

> vccv      vccv
> pencil      index
> vccv
> window
>
> vccv

**12.** Divide the following words into syllables:

       <u>vc/cv</u>
*Example:* pic/nic

        *pencil*             *index*

        *window*

> vc cv      vc cv
> pen/cil      in/dex
> vc cv
> win/dow

**13.** What do you notice about where you divided the words in items 11 and 12? You divided the words _____ the consonants.

> between

**14.** Complete the following generalization:
When a word has the pattern <u>vccv</u>, you usually divide the word _____ the _____ .
Another way of stating this generalization is:
Divide a word after the _____ consonant when the word has a _____ pattern.

> between     consonants
>
> first
> vccv

**15.** To which of the following words does this generalization apply?
*paper   picnic   signal   even   pony   wander*

_____    _____    _____

> picnic    signal    wander

| | |
|---|---|
| **16.** Double consonants in the <u>vccv</u> pattern signal possible exceptions to the <u>vccv</u> generalization. | |
| For example, note that the words *ladder*, *dagger*, *letter*, and *butter* fit the <u>vccv</u> pattern. If these words were divided between the two identical consonants as *lad/der*, *dag/ger*, *let/ter*, and *but/ter*, there might be the tendency to produce two phonemes for the double letter. | |
| If the words were divided into _____ as *ladd/er*, *dagg/er*, *lett/er*, and *butt/er*, only one phoneme would be associated with the double letter. There is variance in how dictionaries divide such words into syllables. | syllables |
| **17.** However, words such as *midday* and *overrate* do follow the <u>vccv</u> generalization because both of the middle consonants are _____ . This is because these words are _____ words. | pronounced    compound |

### 📖 Syllabication Generalization Number 4 (<u>v/cv</u> or <u>vc/v</u>)

| | |
|---|---|
| **18.** Divide the following words into syllables: | |
| *begin* _____     *acorn* _____ <br> *pupil* _____     *over* _____ | be/gin    a/corn <br> pu/pil    o/ver |
| **19.** Mark the vowels and consonants starting with the first vowel and going to the last as shown with *begin*. | |
| $\quad$ vcv <br> *Example:* begin | |
| ‾‾‾           ‾‾‾ <br> *acorn*            *pupil* <br><br> ‾‾ <br> *over* | vcv      vcv <br> acorn    pupil <br><br> vcv <br> over |
| **20.** The words in item 19 have a similar structure. Each word contains the <u>vcv</u> pattern, and you divided the words _____ the first vowel. | after |
| **21.** Complete the following generalization: | |
| When a word has the structure _____ , you usually divide | vcv |
| the word after the _____ vowel. | first |
| Another way of stating this generalization is: | |
| Usually, divide a word _____ the consonant when the | before |
| word pattern is _____ . | vcv |

**22.** To which of the following words does the generalization apply?

*climax*  *lotion*  *seldom*  *silver*  *arbor*  *nasal*

_____  _____  _____

This generalization has two common exceptions, which are presented below.

climax  lotion  nasal

---

**23.** Many words with a vowel followed by a single consonant are divided into syllables after the consonant instead of _____ . Pronounce the following words, then divide them into syllables:

before

*robin*  _____  *rivet*  _____
*limit*  _____  *lemon*  _____
*magic*  _____  *rapid*  _____

rob/in    riv/et
lim/it    lem/on
mag/ic    rap/id

In these words, the consonant following the first vowel is part of the _____ syllable.

first

---

**24.** The words *robot* and *robin* both have the _____ structure. In *robot* the first syllable ends with the vowel; in *robin*, the first syllable ends with the _____ .

vcv

consonant

---

**25.** If you are trying to determine the pronunciation of an unfamiliar word with the <u>vcv</u> structure, remember that the word might be divided into syllables after the first vowel as in *robot* or after the vowel and the _____ as in *robin*.

consonant

---

**26.** The second exception to the <u>vcv</u> generalization can be inferred from the following example. Divide these words into syllables:

*forest*  _____  *chorus*  _____
*miracle*  _____  *sterile*  _____

for/est    chor/us
mir/a/cle  ster/ile

---

**27.** Although Syllabication Generalization Number 4 states that a <u>cvc</u> pattern means that words are usually divided _____ the consonant, this did not apply in the previous example.

before

| | |
|---|---|
| **28.** Look back at item 26 and how you divided the words. What consonant follows the first vowel? _____ | r |
| **29.** Thus, when dividing words according to Syllabication Generalization Number 4, the following must also be considered: When the structure _____ appears in a word and the consonant is an <u>r</u> there can be an exception to Syllabication Generalization Number 4, and the _____ may go with the preceding vowel in the syllable. | vcv<br><br>r |

### 📖 Syllabication Generalization Number 5 (<u>v/digraph v</u> or <u>v/blend v</u>)

| | |
|---|---|
| **30.** Divide the following words into syllables:<br><br>*author* _____     *either* _____<br>*vibrate* _____     *emblem* _____ | au/thor    ei/ther<br>vi/brate   em/blem |
| **31.** The two consonants after the syllable division in these words are either blends or _____ and are _____ divided for syllabication. | digraphs    not |
| **32.** Complete the following generalization:<br>When dividing words into syllables, consonant blends and _____ are generally not _____ . (Note: This can be applied regardless of other structures such as <u>vccv</u> or <u>vcv</u>.) | digraphs    divided |

### 📖 Syllabication Generalization Number 6 (compound words)

| | |
|---|---|
| **33.** Compound words are formed when two words are joined to form a new word. *Birthday, cannot, baseball,* and *drugstore* are all _____ words. | compound |
| **34.** Divide the following words into syllables:<br><br>*birthday* _____     *cannot* _____<br>*baseball* _____     *drugstore* _____<br><br>Did you notice that each _____ is a complete word? | birth/day    can/not<br>base/ball    drug/store<br><br>syllable |

| | |
|---|---|
| **35.** Complete the following generalization.<br><br>When dividing _____ words into syllables, each of the words is a separate _____ or morpheme. | compound<br><br>syllable |

### 📖 Syllabication Generalization Number 7

| | |
|---|---|
| **36.** Divide the following words into syllables:<br><br>   *goodness* _____     *unlock* _____<br>   *regardless* _____   *nonsense* _____ | good/ness   un/lock<br>re/gard/less  non/sense |
| **37.** All of these words contain prefixes or suffixe, i.e.,<br><br>   _____ . | affixes |
| **38.** Are the prefixes and suffixes separate syllables?<br><br>   (yes or no) _____ | yes |
| **39.** Complete the following generalization:<br><br>Prefixes and suffixes are usually separate<br><br>   _____ . | syllables |

### 📖 Syllabication Generalization Number 8 (v/c + le)

| | |
|---|---|
| **40.** The following words end with the two letters<br><br>   _____ .<br><br>   *ankle*    *simple*    *startle*    *needle* | le |
| **41.** Divide these words into syllables:<br><br>   *ankle* _____   *simple* _____<br>   *startle* _____   *needle* _____ | an/kle   sim/ple<br>star/tle  nee/dle |
| **42.** What type of letter appears before the le? (vowel or consonant) _____ | consonant |
| **43.** Look back at the way you divided the words in item 41. The final syllable is composed of the consonant<br><br>plus the _____ . | le |

**44.** Complete the following generalization:

In a word that ends in <u>le</u> preceded by a _____ , the last syllable usually begins with the consonant preceding the

_____ .

This generalization has fairly high utility because most exceptions involve the suffix <u>able</u>.

consonant

le

## ✔ SELF-CHECK FOR SYLLABICATION

**1.**

|  | Divide Words | Number of Syllables |  |  |
|---|---|---|---|---|
| *silent* | _____ | _____ | si/lent | two |
| *helmet* | _____ | _____ | hel/met | two |
| *demon* | _____ | _____ | de/mon | two |
| *Arab* | _____ | _____ | Ar/ab | two |
| *bismuth* | _____ | _____ | bis/muth | two |
| *arable* | _____ | _____ | ar/a/ble | three |
| *lentil* | _____ | _____ | len/til | two |

**2.** What is the visual clue to each syllable division; that is, what pattern can you see?

| *Example: silent* | <u>vcv</u> |  |  |  |
|---|---|---|---|---|
| *helmet* | _____ |  | vccv |  |
| *demon* | _____ |  | vcv |  |
| *Arab* | _____ |  | vrv |  |
| *bismuth* | _____ |  | vccv |  |
| *arable* | _____ | _____ | vrv | ble |
| *lentil* | _____ |  | vccv |  |

## 📖📖 Using Syllabication to Help with Pronunciation

**1.** One purpose for dividing words into syllables is to arrive at smaller pronunciation units. Determining the appropriate

_____ sounds within syllables can aid in _____ and thus help in decoding a word. Pronunciation generalizations are concerned with appropriate division of words into syllables and the establishment of the vowel _____ in each syllable.

vowel          pronunciation

sound

| | |
|---|---|
| 2. As you work toward the pronunciation of an unfamiliar word often you will come close to its _____ , yet not produce the exact, "correct" pronunciation. However, approximations of the correct pronunciation can be very useful if the word is part of your oral vocabulary because often other clues will act _____ with the approximation to help you determine the correct pronunciation of the word. | pronunciation<br><br><br><br>together |
| 3. Before we begin, here are two definitions that will be useful as you read through the section. First, *closed syllables* are _____ that contain one vowel and end in a consonant, such as *sun* or *sig/nal.* Second, *open syllables* are syllables that end in a vowel, such as *me* or *be/gin.* | syllables |

### 📖 Pronunciation Generalization Number 1

| | |
|---|---|
| 4. Do the following words end with a (vowel or consonant)? _____<br><br>*get        pin        ran        sun        rot* | consonant |
| 5. In these words, does the vowel sound long (glided) or short (unglided)? _____<br><br>*get        pin        ran        sun        rot* | short (unglided) |
| 6. Recall that syllables containing one vowel and ending with a consonant are called _____ syllables. | closed |
| 7. Complete the following generalization:<br>Closed syllables usually contain _____ , or unglided, vowel sounds.<br>This generalization also applies to syllables in words of more than one syllable:<br><br>*picnic*    pic/nic                    *signal*    sig/nal | short |

## Pronunciation Generalization Number 2

| | |
|---|---|
| **8.** What is the sound of the vowel in the following words? (long or glided; short or unglided). _____<br><br>*high   night   kind   find   cold   told* | long (glided) |
| **9.** Are the words in item 8 closed syllables? (yes or no)<br><br>_____ | yes |
| **10.** Write the vowel and the two letters that follow it:<br><br>*high         night         _____*<br>*find         kind         _____*<br>*cold         told         _____*<br><br>These are letter structures that call for long vowel sounds in<br><br>(open or closed) _____ syllables. | igh<br>ind<br>old<br><br><br>closed |
| **11.** Complete the following generalization:<br>When the structures i<u>gh</u>, <u>old</u>, and _____ appear in a<br>word, the vowel sound is usually _____ , even though the<br>syllable is closed. | ind<br>long (glided) |

## Pronunciation Generalization Number 3

| | |
|---|---|
| **12.** In the following words, are the underlined syllables closed? (yes or no) _____<br><br><u>for</u> est   <u>thir</u> sty   <u>pur</u> suit   <u>car</u> toon<br>What letter follows the first vowel in each word? _____ | yes<br><br><br>r |
| **13.** Is the first vowel in the underlined syllables in item 12 long or short? _____ | neither (r-controlled) |
| **14.** Complete the following generalization:<br>The consonant _____ following a vowel usually creates a<br>closed syllable but may result in an _____ vowel sound.<br>This can be viewed as another exception to the closed syllable<br>generalization (Pronunciation Generalization Number 1). | r<br>r-controlled |

## Pronunciation Generalization Number 4

| | |
|---|---|
| **15.** The last letter in the following words is a _____ . (vowel or consonant)<br><br>   *be*        *go*        *me* | vowel |
| **16.** Are the vowel sounds in the words in item 15 long (glided) or short (unglided)? _____ | long (glided) |
| **17.** Recall that syllables are called _____ syllables when a vowel is the last letter in the _____ .<br>This generalization applies to syllables in words of more than one syllable:<br><br>o̱ pen<br><br>be̱ gin<br><br>la̱ zy<br><br>pu̱ pil | open<br>syllable |
| **18.** Complete the following generalization:<br>Open syllables usually end with _____ vowel sounds. | long (glided) |

## Pronunciation Generalization Number 5

| | |
|---|---|
| **19.** Recall that two vowels appearing side by side usually represent _____ vowel sound, as seen in the following words:<br><br> *pain*    *read*    *pail*    *seek* | one |
| **20.** This generalization also applies to words of more than one syllable, as shown below.<br>Pronounce the following words:<br><br> *teacher*     *obtain*     *detail*     *moaning*<br>How many vowels are there in these words?<br><br>_____<br><br>How many vowel sounds? _____ | three<br>two |

| | |
|---|---|
| 21. Complete the following generalization:<br>Two vowels together usually indicate that the first one is long and the second one is _____ , unless the vowel combination is a vowel diphthong or a variant vowel _____ . | silent<br><br>digraph |

### 📖 Pronunciation Generalization Number 6

| | |
|---|---|
| 22. Recall that a final <u>e</u> preceded by a single consonant usually indicates that the preceding vowel is _____ with the <u>e</u> itself being _____ (or a marker). Thus, the pattern of the following words calls for _____ vowel sound. (one or more than one)<br><br>    *ate*        *cake*       *hope*      *kite*<br><br>This generalization also _____ to words of more than one syllable.<br>Pronounce the following words (noticing the last syllable):<br>imi<u>tate</u>      graph<u>ite</u>     tele<u>scope</u>    a<u>wake</u> | long<br>silent<br>one<br><br><br><br>applies |
| 23. Complete the following generalization:<br>When a word ends in <u>e</u> preceded by a single consonant, the vowel before the consonant is usually _____ . | long |
| 24. Pronounce the following words. Notice that they all end in <u>e</u>.<br>   *fence*      *dance*     *sledge*<br>Is the first vowel long or short? _____<br>How many consonants are between the first vowel and the final <u>e</u>? _____<br>When a word ends in <u>e</u> but is not preceded by a single consonant, the final <u>e</u> may be silent but does not affect the preceding _____ sound. | short<br><br>two<br><br><br>vowel |

**SELF-CHECK FOR PRONUNCIATION GENERALIZATIONS**

1.  Indicate the vowel sounds in the following words:

*Example:* sup          short <u>u</u>

find          _____

soften        _____          _____

gain          _____          _____

journey       _____          _____

sparkle       _____          _____

dance         _____          _____

token         _____          _____

long i
short o          short e
long a           silent i
r-controlled u   short e
short a          schwa
short a          silent e
long o           short e

# Using the Dictionary

Dictionaries are used as a reference for confirming and studying meanings, pronunciations, and spellings of words. They are considered useful to readers who are trying to determine the meaning and pronunciation of unfamiliar words. They are also useful as a strategy for word analysis. Dictionaries can be used at all grade levels, beginning with picture dictionaries at the earliest levels and moving to specialized, subject-specific dictionaries that are appropriate for older readers.

Most dictionaries intended for middle school grades and higher contain much useful information in addition to the main word entries, pronunciation entries, and definitions that appear in the body of the dictionary. Examples of information in a dictionary, usually after all of the main entries have been presented, might include listings of colleges and universities in the United States, proofreader's markings and terms, abbreviations used in writing, and tables of weights and measures. However, we limit the discussion in this chapter to the use of a dictionary to help in word analysis. Therefore, our focus is on understanding the organization and key features of dictionaries as a means to this end.

 **LOCATING WORDS IN A DICTIONARY**

1. Using a dictionary can be a helpful word analysis strategy. Usually, however, dictionaries are used only when pronunciation generalizations, structural _____ , and context clues are not effective.

   analysis

2. To use a dictionary, a child must know how to alphabetize by at least the _____ letter of a word.

   first

3. In addition, to use a dictionary effectively, a reader must be aware that a word often has more than one _____ and must be able to use context to select one meaning from alternatives.

   meaning

4. Guide words appear at the top of each page in the body of a dictionary and help readers to locate particular words quickly. The _____ word on the left side of the page indicates the first word on that page. The guide word on the right side of the page indicates the _____ word on that page.

   guide

   last

5. By using knowledge of the position of letters in the _____ , readers can determine whether a word is on a particular page, on a preceding page, or on a subsequent page.

   alphabet

6. Try the following activity. Given the set of boldface guide words, indicate whether the word to be located is on that page, on a preceding page, or on a subsequent page.

   **citizen**          **clamp**

   | Words to be located | *civil* | _____ | on |
   | | *clairvoyance* | _____ | on |
   | | *clan* | _____ | subsequent |
   | | *city* | _____ | on |
   | | *choice* | _____ | preceding |

   **lumbago**          **lurid**

   | Words to be located | *lurk* | _____ | subsequent |
   | | *lunge* | _____ | on |
   | | *lucid* | _____ | preceding |
   | | *lumper* | _____ | on |
   | | *lugger* | _____ | preceding |

| | |
|---|---|
| 7. Once a particular word has been located, dictionaries provide several types of information. <u>For most words, _____ specify pronunciation, parts of speech, syllabication, word derivation, and meaning(s).</u> | dictionaries |

 **USING A DICTIONARY TO HELP DETERMINE PRONUNCIATION**

| | |
|---|---|
| 8. The entry following the main entry word is the pronunciation entry. The _____ entry is always in parentheses. For example, if the main entry word is *mimic*, you would see: **mim·ic** (mim′ik) *n.* In this case, *mim′ik* is the _____ entry for the word *mimic*. The "*n.*" following the pronunciation entry indicates that this entry defines *mimic* as a _____ . | pronunciation

pronunciation

noun |
| 9. Notice that the information provided for the main entry word *mimic* includes information about how to pronounce the main entry word, how the main entry word should be divided into _____ , which syllable should be accented, and what is the main entry word's part of _____ . | syllables
speech |
| 10. Parts of speech are indicated immediately after the pronunciation parentheses. They are always abbreviated; for example, *n.* = noun, *adj.* = adjective. These _____ vary slightly in various dictionaries. | abbreviations |
| 11. Dictionaries use diacritical marks and key words to indicate pronunciation. _____ marks indicate stress or accents of syllables within words and show vowel _____ as being either long (glided) or short (unglided). The common diacritical marks are shown below:

  ′   used to indicate stress or accent
  -   used above a vowel to indicate a long vowel sound
  ˘   used above a vowel to indicate a short vowel sound | Diacritical
pronunciations |

| | |
|---|---|
| **12.** Dictionaries provide a pronunciation guide at the bottom of each page. When readers are unsure about a diacritical mark or the pronunciation of a particular letter or letter combination, they can use the _____ guide. | pronunciation |
| **13.** At the bottom of a dictionary page, you can find examples for each _____ mark and key words for help with _____ . For more help with pronunciation, detailed pronunciation information appears in the front of a dictionary—usually on the page just before the word entries begin. It will be labeled *Pronunciation Key*. The Pronunciation _____ contains precise information on dictionary use and pronunciation. | diacritical          pronunciation<br><br><br><br>Key |
| **14.** Information about accent marks, syllabication, and sound-letter correspondences is included in _____ dictionary entry. If the entry contains more than one accent mark, one accent mark will be darker than the other. The syllable before the _____ accent mark gets more emphasis.<br>Some words are spelled the same way but are pronounced differently. Sometimes, the differences in the pronunciation of words is related to which syllable is _____ . | each (every)<br><br><br>darker<br><br><br>accented (emphasized) |
| **15.** Dictionaries are not all consistent in the way that they mark short vowels. In some dictionaries, the _____ vowel sound is not marked at all. Readers need to consult their respective dictionary's _____ key. | short<br><br>pronunciation |
| **16.** At times, only a portion of a word will be found in the parentheses containing the _____ entry. This occurs for two reasons. First, a particular word might be followed by several words that use part of the main entry word. Here are entries for the word *milk* and words that use the word *milk*.<br>**milk** (mĭlk)<br>**milk fish** (-fĭsh′)<br>**milkman** (-măn′)<br>**milkmaid** (-mād′)<br>In these instances, the pronunciation for the first part of each word (milk) is assumed. Readers should look back to the first, or main _____ for the pronunciation of the assumed part. | pronunciation<br><br><br><br><br><br><br><br><br><br>entry |

| | |
|---|---|
| **17.** The second reason for an incomplete entry is that some dictionaries do not provide pronunciation for common affixes, such as -<u>ing</u>, -<u>er</u>, -<u>ful</u>, and -<u>ness</u>. Those dictionaries will have these _____ as main entries. Such main entries will appear with a dash in front of them to indicate that they are not complete _____ , for example, -<u>ing</u>. | affixes<br><br><br>words |
| **18.** At times, a word might have more than one acceptable pronunciation. For example, *data* can be pronounced two different ways, with the first vowel being either _____ or long. If there is more than one pronunciation shown in the entry, both are acceptable. The first one, however, is _____ . | short<br><br>preferred |

## USING A DICTIONARY TO HELP DETERMINE MEANING

| | |
|---|---|
| **19.** In addition to _____ , dictionaries also help a reader to determine a word's meaning by providing common definitions for each main entry. _____ usually appear after the word's part of speech has been given, for example, after it has been designated as a noun, verb, adjective, or adverb. | pronunciation<br><br>Definitions |
| **20.** For words that have only one definition, the use of a dictionary to help a reader determine meaning is quite simple. For example, in one common school dictionary, the word *migrant* has only one definition. For other words, however, there may be two or more _____ . | definitions |
| **21.** In some dictionaries, the word *bank* has three main _____ : one for the bank that deals with money, one for a mound of dirt, and one for a row or tier of something. When coming upon a number of definitions for a main entry word, readers must make a _____ between one of the possible definitions and the original context in which the _____ occurred. | entries<br><br><br><br>match<br>word |

| | |
|---|---|
| **22.** Definitions are usually placed in order from the most common to the least frequently used meaning. A definition needs to be linked to the context from which the word came. Beginning readers often need to be taught that it is not appropriate to use the first _____ that appears without checking the original _____ . | definition<br><br>context |
| **23.** Dictionaries often offer additional information that helps a reader to understand the meaning and _____ of words. Entries might contain labels such as *slang*, *obsolete*, and *colloquial*. These labels provide extra insights into how particular words are used. | usage |
| **24.** When entries provide synonyms, the abbreviation **SYN.** is used. **SYN.** is easy to locate because it appears in dark print and is _____ . When it is appropriate, most dictionaries provide information about word derivation. When words have spelling changes due to inflected endings, these _____ are also provided. For example, the main entry *make* would appear as **make** (māk), **made, making.** | capitalized<br><br><br>spellings |

✔ ### SELF-CHECK FOR CHAPTER NINE

| | |
|---|---|
| **1.** If the entry guide words are **island** and **isolate,** which word would appear on the right side of the page? _____<br>Which word would appear on the left side of the page? _____ | isolate<br><br><br>island |
| **2.** Using these same guide words, would the following words appear on that page, on a preceding page, or on a subsequent page?<br>  *isobar*   _____<br>  *irritable*   _____<br>  *isthmus*   _____<br>  *isoglass*   _____<br>  *island*   _____<br>  *isoprene*   _____ | on<br>preceding<br>subsequent<br>on<br>on<br>subsequent |
| **3.** For the entry: mon·ey (mŭn′ e) *n.*<br>What part of speech is it?   _____<br>How would you pronounce <u>ey</u>?   _____<br>Which syllable is accented?   _____ | noun<br>long e<br>first |

**4.** For the entry: lac·tose (lak′ tos) *n.*

What is the vowel sound for the <u>o</u> in lactose? _____     long o

What is the consonant sound for the <u>c</u>? _____     hard c (or k)

Which syllable is accented? _____     first

**5.** When an entry has multiple meanings listed, readers must check

the _____ where they encountered the word to determine     context

the appropriate _____ .     meaning (or definition)

**6.** The first definition found in an entry indicates the meaning for

the most _____ usage.     common

**7.** The abbreviation **SYN.** indicates that _____ will follow.     synonyms 同義字

# Posttest I

Take this posttest and then compare your answers with the answers provided on pages 110–112.

1. On a separate sheet of paper, define the following central terms that are important in understanding word analysis principles:
   - phoneme
   - grapheme
   - phonemic awareness
   - phonological awareness
   - onset patterns
   - rime patterns
   - consonant digraph
   - consonant blend
   - context clues
   - sight words
   - phonetic phase
   - semiphonetic phase
   - precommunicative phase
   - morpheme
   - affix
   - closed syllables
   - open syllables
   - pronunciation entry

2. Readers use word _____ strategies to analyze written words in order to construct both their sounds and their meanings.

3. The spoken word *mast* has _____ phonemes

4. The spoken word *ship* has _____ phonemes

5. Context clues may assist readers with both _____ and _____ .

6. A close relationship between the letters and sounds in a language is referred to as the _____ principle.

7. In kindergarten, the best single predictor of later reading success is a child's level of _____ awareness.

8. In English, _____ represent the most consistent letter-sound relationships.

9. The onset letter <u>c</u> usually represents the sound associated with the letter <u>s</u> when it is followed by the vowel letters _____ , _____ , and _____ . We refer to this as the " _____ <u>c</u>" sound.

10. Approximately 200 of the most common words account for about _____ percent of the words in most reading selections.

11. Short _____ sounds often appear in a syllable or single-syllable word that ends in a consonant or consonant cluster.

12. _____ vowels are neither long nor short. They have a sound determined by the _____ <u>r</u>.

13. <u>Y</u> represents a vowel sound when it appears at the _____ of a word.

14. A digraph represents _____ sound. A _____ represents a blending of two vowel sounds.

15. A _____ vowel sound is usually produced when two vowels appear side by side.

16. Words that are recognized and pronounced automatically are called _____ words.

**17.** Match the vowel sound represented by the underlined letter(s) in the words in Column A with the type of vowel sound in Column B by placing the number of the type of vowel sound in Column B in the space in front of the word in Column A.

| A | B |
|---|---|
| _____ egg | 1. long (glided) |
| _____ go | 2. short (unglided) |
| _____ side | 3. "r"-controlled |
| _____ joy | 4. diphthong |
| _____ low | |
| _____ cord | |
| _____ cheap | |
| _____ begin | |
| _____ pout | |
| _____ lap | |

**18.** Place an L in the space in front of the word in Column A if the underlined vowel represents the long sound and an S if it represents a short sound. Then select the reason for the vowel sound in Column B and place the appropriate number in the space behind the word in Column A.

| A | | B |
|---|---|---|
| _____ begin | _____ | 1. final e |
| _____ pencil | _____ | 2. vowel digraph |
| _____ pain | _____ | 3. open syllable |
| _____ rope | _____ | 4. closed syllable |
| _____ preacher | _____ | |
| _____ digraph | _____ | |
| _____ simple | _____ | |
| _____ fate | _____ | |

**19.** Match the principle for syllabication in Column B with the word in Column A by placing the number of the visual clue in the space in front of the word in Column A.

| A | B |
|---|---|
| _____ turtle | 1. v/cv |
| _____ unclear | 2. vc/cv |
| _____ airtight | 3. vc/(blend) v |
| _____ overt | 4. vr/v |
| _____ oral | 5. /c-le |
| _____ mental | 6. compound word |
| _____ simple | 7. prefix |
| _____ belongs | |
| _____ preview | |
| _____ football | |
| _____ peril | |
| _____ hundred | |

**20.** If the guide words for a page in the dictionary were *protreptic* and *proximate*, indicate whether the following words would appear:

- *on that page* by writing **on** in the space in front of the word.
- *on a following page* by writing **follow** in the space in front of the word.
- *before the page* by writing **before** in the space in front of the word.

| | | | |
|---|---|---|---|
| _____ protostele | | _____ psaltery | |
| _____ provisory | | _____ prove | |
| _____ preview | | _____ protozoan | |
| _____ provost | | _____ protractor | |
| _____ prude | | | |

## ANSWERS TO POSTTEST I

**1.** Definitions

| | |
|---|---|
| *phoneme* | A phoneme is the smallest single unit of sound in a language that distinguishes one *morpheme* (meaning unit) from another. (Chapters 1 and 2) |
| *grapheme* | A grapheme is a written or printed representation of a phoneme. (Chapter 1) |
| *phonemic awareness* | Phonemic awareness is the awareness of individual sounds or phonemes as objects that can be analyzed and manipulated. (Chapters 1 and 2) |
| *phonological awareness* | Phonological awareness is the awareness of individual words and syllables as objects that can be analyzed and manipulated. (Chapters 1 and 2) |
| *onset patterns* | Onset patterns include initial consonant letters found at the *beginning* of syllables and words such as <u>b</u>, <u>c</u>, <u>d</u>, <u>f</u>, <u>g</u>, <u>sn</u>, <u>st</u>, or <u>str</u>. (Chapter 3) |
| *rime patterns* | Rime patterns include a limited set of the most common *endings* to syllables and words such as -<u>ake</u>, -<u>ack</u>, -<u>ail</u>, or -<u>ame</u>. (Chapter 3) |
| *consonant digraph* | Consonant digraphs are two different consonant letters that appear together and represent a single sound, or phoneme, not usually associated with either letter. (Chapter 3) |
| *consonant blend* | A consonant blend consists of two or three consecutive consonant letters, each representing a separate phoneme that is blended together. (Chapter 3) |
| *context clues* | Context clues consist of the information around a word that provides assistance in determining its pronunciation and meaning. (Chapter 5) |
| *sight words* | Sight words are words recognized automatically without conscious attention. (Chapter 6) |
| *phonetic phase* | A phase in developmental spelling where writing looks like a child is trying to represent nearly every sound in each word by spelling it as it sounds. (Chapter 7) |

| | |
|---|---|
| *semiphonetic phase* | A phase in developmental spelling where children use writing to communicate meaning but words are represented often only by the initial letter sound. More consonants than vowels appear. (Chapter 7) |
| *precommunicative phase* | A phase in developmental spelling where writing is characterized by not having a consistent communicative intent. (Chapter 7) |
| *morpheme* | The smallest unit of meaning in a language. (Chapter 8) |
| *affix* | A prefix or a suffix. (Chapter 8) |
| *closed syllables* | A syllable ending with a consonant letter, usually making the vowel sound short. (Chapter 4) |
| *open syllables* | A syllable ending with a vowel letter, usually making the vowel sound long. (Chapter 4) |
| *pronunciation entry* | The entry in a dictionary that provides information about a word's pronunciation. (Chapter 9) |

2. analysis (Chapter 1)

3. four (Chapter 2)

4. three (Chapter 2)

5. pronunciation    meaning (Chapter 5)

6. alphabetic (Chapter 2)

7. phonemic (Chapter 7)

8. consonants (Chapter 3)

9. e    i    y    soft (Chapter 3)

10. 50 (Chapter 6)

11. vowel (Chapter 4)

12. R-controlled    following (Chapter 4)

13. end (Chapter 4)

14. one    blend (diphthong) (Chapter 4)

15. long (Chapter 4)

16. sight (Chapter 6)

17. Matching vowels (Chapter 4)

2 egg

1 go

1 side

4 joy

4 low

3 cord

1 cheap

2 begin

4 pout

2 lap

**18.** Long and short vowels (Chapter 4)

| | | |
|---|---|---|
| L | begin | 3 |
| S | pencil | 4 |
| L | pain | 2 |
| L | rope | 1 |
| L | preacher | 2 |
| L | digraph | 3 |
| S | simple | 4 |
| L | fate | 1 |

**19.** Syllabication (Chapter 8)

5 turtle

7 unclear

6 airtight

1 overt

4 oral

2 mental

5 simple

1 belongs

7 preview

6 football

4 peril

3 hundred

**20.** Dictionary guide words (Chapter 9)

| | |
|---|---|
| before | protostele |
| on | provisory |
| before | preview |
| on | provost |
| follow | prude |
| follow | psaltery |
| on | prove |
| before | protozoan |
| before | protractor |

# Posttest II

Take this posttest and then compare your answers with the answers provided on pages 116-118.

1. On a separate sheet of paper, define the following central terms that are important to understanding word analysis principles:
   - diphthong
   - graphophonic
   - phonemic awareness
   - prefix
   - cvc pattern
   - vowel
   - grapheme
   - inflectional ending
   - morpheme
   - phonics
   - orthography
   - consonant cluster
   - _r_-controlled vowel
   - semiphonetic phase
   - alphabetic principle
   - word analysis strategies
   - guide words
   - closed syllable

**2.** Which of the following is the best predictor of later reading success for kindergarten children? _____

    (a) graphophonic knowledge

    (b) phonemic awareness

    (c) phonic knowledge

**3.** Context clues assist readers in predicting and confirming meaning, but pronunciation is accessed through word analysis clues other than context. (True or false?) _____

**4.** What are the four types of clues authors provide that readers can use as context clues? _____ , _____ , _____ , and _____

**5.** The spoken word *poles* has _____ morphemes.

**6.** The spoken word *poles* has _____ phonemes.

**7.** The written word *poles* has _____ graphemes.

**8.** The written word *poles* has _____ alphabetic letters.

**9.** Approximately 400 of the most common words account for about _____ percent of the words in most reading selections.

**10.** A digraph represents _____ sound. A _____ represents a blending of two vowel sounds.

**11.** High-frequency words are usually also _____ _____ for most readers.

**12.** Match the vowel sound represented by the underlined letter(s) in the words in Column A with the type of vowel sound in Column B by placing the number of the type of vowel sound in Column B in the space in front of the word in Column A.

| A | B |
|---|---|
| _____ am | 1. long(glided) |
| _____ me | 2. short (unglided) |
| _____ pride | 3. "r" controlled |
| _____ toy | 4. diphthong |
| _____ glow | |
| _____ bird | |
| _____ beat | |
| _____ slim | |
| _____ pout | |
| _____ lap | |

**13.** Place an <u>L</u> in the space in front of the word in Column A if the underlined vowel represents the long sound and an <u>S</u> if it represents a short sound. Then select the reason for the vowel sound in Column B and place the appropriate number in the space behind the word in Column A.

| **A** | | **B** |
|---|---|---|
| _____ t<u>o</u>ken | _____ | 1. final <u>e</u> |
| _____ l<u>e</u>ntil | _____ | 2. vowel digraph |
| _____ r<u>ai</u>n | _____ | 3. open syllable |
| _____ sl<u>o</u>pe | _____ | 4. closed syllable |
| _____ t<u>ea</u>cher | _____ | |
| _____ d<u>i</u>graph | _____ | |
| _____ d<u>i</u>mple | _____ | |
| _____ g<u>a</u>te | _____ | |

**14.** Match the principle for syllabication in Column B with the word in Column A by placing the number of the visual clue in the space in front of the word in Column A.

| **A** | **B** |
|---|---|
| _____ castle | 1. v/cv |
| _____ undo | 2. vc/cv |
| _____ staircase | 3. vc/(blend) v |
| _____ open | 4. vr/v |
| _____ army | 5. /c-le |
| _____ magma | 6. compound word |
| _____ dimple | 7. prefix |
| _____ cement | |
| _____ return | |
| _____ doorway | |
| _____ urban | |
| _____ hundred | |

**15.** If the guide words for a page in the dictionary were *ethic* and *eucaryotic*, indicate whether the following words would appear:
- *on that page* by writing **on** in the space in front of the word.
- *on a following page* by writing **follow** in the space in front of the word.
- *before the page* by writing **before** in the space in front of the word.

| | |
|---|---|
| _____ eternity | _____ euglenoid |
| _____ etiquette | _____ ethmoid |
| _____ ethereal | _____ etching |
| _____ etiology | _____ etcetera |
| _____ eugenic | |

**16.** Being able to identify the initial consonant sound in a word like *sit* is an example of _____ awareness.

17. Being able to clap each syllable in a word is an example of
_____ _____ .

    (a) phonemic awareness

    (b) phonological awareness

    (c) syllabication awareness

18. The onset letter <u>c</u> usually represents the sound associated with the letter <u>k</u> when it is followed by the vowel letters _____ , _____ , and _____ .

19. When dividing compound words into syllables, each word is usually its own syllable. (True or false?) _____

20. If a word ends in <u>le</u>, explain the process you would use to decide on that word's last syllable.

## ANSWERS TO POSTTEST II

1. Definitions

| | |
|---|---|
| *diphthong* | A type of vowel cluster that is sometimes called a vowel blend, where two vowel letters appear together and represent a blending of the sounds associated with each letter. (Chapter 4) |
| *graphophonic* | Describes the relationship between sounds in our language and its written letters or spelling patterns. (Chapter 1) |
| *phonemic awareness* | Phonemic awareness is the awareness of individual sounds or phonemes as objects that can be analyzed and manipulated. (Chapters 1 and 2) |
| *prefix* | An affix added to the beginning of root words to change their meanings. (Chapter 8) |
| *vcv pattern* | A vowel-consonant-vowel pattern. A generalization for syllabication that suggests the division appear after the first vowel in the pattern. (Chapter 8) |
| *vowel* | Sounds produced without a restriction in the airstream, represented by the five letters <u>a</u>, <u>e</u>, <u>i</u>, <u>o</u>, <u>u</u>, and sometimes <u>y</u> and <u>w</u>. (Chapter 4) |
| *grapheme* | A grapheme is a written or printed representation of a phoneme. (Chapter 1) |
| *inflectional ending* | An affix added to the end of a root word; often changes the grammatical function but not the core meaning of the root word to which it is added. (Chapter 8) |
| *morpheme* | The smallest unit of meaning in a language. (Chapters 1 and 8) |
| *phonics* | Phonics refers to the application of information about the sounds of language to the teaching of reading and to the knowledge about how sounds are represented by letters or letter combinations in written language to help readers determine the oral equivalents of unfamiliar words. (Chapter 1) |
| *orthography* | The writing system of a language. (Chapter 1) |

| | |
|---|---|
| *consonant cluster* | Consonant clusters include two or three consonant letters that often appear together. There are two types: digraphs and blends. (Chapter 3) |
| *r-controlled vowel* | R-controlled vowels are neither long nor short but have a sound determined largely by the following r. (Chapters 4 and 8) |
| *semiphonetic phase* | A phase in developmental spelling where children use writing to communicate meaning but words are represented often only by the initial letter sound. More consonants than vowels appear. (Chapter 7) |
| *alphabetic principle* | Knowledge about the close relationship between the letters and sounds in a language. (Chapter 2 and 7) |
| *word analysis strategies* | Strategies that permit you to determine both the sounds of words and their meanings. Word analysis strategies include phonological and phonemic awareness, phonics, context use, sight word knowledge, morphemic and structural analysis, and dictionary skills. (Chapter 1) |
| *guide words* | Guide words appear at the top of each page in the body of a dictionary and help readers to locate particular words quickly. (Chapter 9) |
| *closed syllable* | A syllable ending with a consonant letter, usually making the vowel sound short. (Chapters 4 and 8) |

2. (b) phonemic awareness (Chapters 1 and 2)

3. False (Chapter 5)

4. definition, synonym, example, and mood (Chapter 5)

5. two (Chapters 1 and 8)

6. four (Chapters 1 and 8)

7. four (Chapters 1 and 8)

8. five (Chapters 1 and 8)

9. 70 (Chapter 6)

10. one blend (diphthong). (Chapter 4)

11. sight words (Chapter 6)

12. Matching vowels (Chapter 4)

    2 am

    1 me

    1 pride

    4 toy

    4 glow

    3 bird

    1 beat

    2 slim

    4 pout

    2 lap

**13.** Long and short vowels (Chapter 4)

L token    3

S lentil    4

L rain    2

L slope    1

L teacher 2

L digraph 3

S dimple  4

L gate    1

**14.** Syllabication (Chapter 8)

5 castle

7 undo

6 staircase

1 open

4 army

2 magma

5 dimple

1 cement

7 return

6 doorway

2 urban

3 hundred

**15.** Dictionary guide words (Chapter 9)

before    eternity

on        etiquette

before    ethereal

on        etiology

follow    eugenic

follow    euglenoid

on        ethmoid

before    etching

before    etcetera

**16.** phonemic (Chapter 2)

**17.** phonological awareness (Chapter 2)

**18.** o, a, u (Chapter 3)

**19.** True (Chapter 8)

**20.** If the letter before the <u>le</u> is a consonant, the consonant plus <u>le</u> form the last syllable. (Chapter 8)

# References

Included in this section are references that contain suggestions for teaching word analysis strategies to children, references that provide additional information about English orthography, references that examine issues related to word analysis, and references that report research related to word analysis and spelling. Some older references are included because they are classic works and still inform the field.

Adams, M. J. (1990). *Beginning to read: Thinking and learning about print.* Cambridge, MA: MIT Press.

Adams, M. J., Foorman, B. R., Lundberg, I., & Beeler, T. (1998). *Phonemic awareness in young children.* Baltimore, MD: Paul H. Brookes.

Anderson, R. C., Hiebert, E. H., Scott, J. A., & Wilkinson, I. A. G. (1985). *Becoming a nation of readers.* Washington, DC: National Institute of Education.

Bailey, M. H. (1967). The utility of phonic generalizations in grades one through six. *The Reading Teacher, 22,* 413–418.

Baumann, J. F., Hoffman, J. V., Moon, J., & Duffy-Hester, A. M. (1998). Where are teachers' voices in the phonics/whole language debate? Results from a survey of U.S. elementary classroom teachers. *The Reading Teacher, 51,* 636–650.

Bear, D. R. (Ed.) (1999). *Words their way:* Word study for phonics, vocabulary, and spelling instruction (2nd ed.). Upper Saddle River, NJ: Prentice Hall.

Bear, D. R., & Templeton, S. (1998). Explorations in developmental spelling: Foundations for learning and teaching phonics, spelling, and vocabulary. *The Reading Teacher, 52,* 222–242.

Burmeister, L. E. (1969). Usefulness of phonics generalizations. *The Reading Teacher, 21*, 349–356.

Canney, G., & Schreiner, R. (1976–1977). A study of the effectiveness of selected syllabication rules and phonogram patterns for word attack. *Reading Research Quarterly, 12*, 102–124.

Chomsky, C. (1970). Reading, writing, and phonology. *Harvard Educational Review, 40*, 287–309.

Clay, M. M. (1991). *Becoming literate: The construction of inner control.* Portsmouth, NH: Heinemann Educational Books.

Clymer, T. (1963). The utility of phonics generalizations in the primary grades. *The Reading Teacher, 16*, 252–258.

Cunningham, P. M. (1991). *Phonics they use: Words for reading and writing.* New York: HarperCollins.

Davidson, J. L. (Ed.). (1988). *Counterpoint and beyond: A response to becoming a nation of readers.* Urbana, IL: National Council of Teachers of English.

Dawson, M. (Ed.). (1971). *Teaching word recognition skills.* Newark, DE: International Reading Association.

Dechant, E. (1993). *Whole-language teaching: A comprehensive teaching guide.* Lancaster, PA: Technomic Publishing.

Dolch, E. W. (1951). *Psychology and teaching of reading.* Champaign, IL: The Gerrard Press.

Duffelmeyer, F. A., & Black, J. L. (1996). The names test: A domain-specific validation study. *The Reading Teacher, 50*, 148–150.

Duffelmeyer, F. A., Kruse, A. E., Merkley, D. J., & Fyfe, S. A. (1994). Further validation and enhancement of the names test. *The Reading Teacher, 48*, 118–128.

Durkin, D. (1974). Phonics: Instruction that needs to be improved. *The Reading Teacher, 28*, 152–157.

———. (1981). *Strategies for identifying words.* Boston, MA: Allyn & Bacon.

Emans, R. (1967). The usefulness of phonic generalizations above the primary grades. *The Reading Teacher, 20*, 419–425.

Emans, R., & Harms, J. M. (1973). The usefulness of linguistically based word generalizations. *Reading World, 13*, 13–21.

Ericson, L., & Juiebo, M. F. (1998). *The phonological awareness handbook for kindergarten and primary teachers.* Newark, DE: International Reading Association.

Freppon, P. A., & Dahl, K. L. (1991). Learning about phonics in a whole language classroom. *Language Arts, 68*, 190–197.

Frith, U. (Ed.). (1979). *Cognitive processes in spelling.* New York: Academic Press.

Fry, E. B. (1980). The new instant word list. *The Reading Teacher, 34*, 284–289.

Gillet, J. W., & Temple, C. (1994). *Understanding reading problems: Assessment and instruction* (4th ed.). Glenview, IL: Scott Foresman.

Goodman, K. S. (1993). *Phonics facts*. Portsmouth, NH: Heinemann Educational Books.

————. (1986). *What's whole in whole language?* Portsmouth, NH: Heinemann Educational Books.

Groff, P. (1998). Where's the phonics? Making a case for its direct and systematic instruction. *The Reading Teacher, 52*, 138–142.

————. (1973). Fifteen flaws of phonics. *Elementary English, 50*, 35–40.

Gunning, T. G. (1995). Word building: A strategic approach to the teaching of phonics. *The Reading Teacher, 48*, 484–488.

Hanna, P., Hodges, R. E., & Hanna, J. S. (1971). *Spelling: Structure and strategies*. Boston, MA: Houghton Mifflin.

Heilman, A. (1989). *Phonics in proper perspective* (6th ed.). Upper Saddle River, NJ: Merrill/Prentice Hall.

Henderson, E. H., & Beers, J. W. (Eds.). (1982). *Developmental and cognitive aspects of learning to spell*. Newark, DE: International Reading Association.

Hull, M. A. *Phonics for the teacher of reading*, (4th ed.). Columbus, OH: Merrill.

Johnson, D. D., & Merryman, E. (1971). Syllabication: The erroneous VCCV generalization. *The Reading Teacher, 25*, 267–270.

Johnson, D. D., & Pearson, D. P. (1984). *Teaching reading vocabulary* (2nd ed.). New York: Holt, Rinehart and Winston.

Lapp, D., & Flood, J. (1997). Where's the phonics? Making the case (again) for integrated code instruction. *The Reading Teacher, 50*, 696–700.

Leu, D. J., Jr., & Kinzer, C. K. (1999). *Effective literacy instruction* (4th ed.). Upper Saddle River, NJ: Prentice Hall.

Morrow, L. M. (1993). *Literacy development in the early years.* (2nd ed.). Boston, MA: Allyn & Bacon.

Morrow, L. M., & Tracey, D. H. (1997). *The Reading Teacher, 50*, 644–651.

Powell, D., & Hornsby, D. (1993). *Learning phonics and spelling in a whole language classroom*. New York: Scholastic Professional Books.

Reiner, K. (1998). Developing a kindergarten phonemic awareness program: An action research project. *The Reading Teacher, 52*, 70–73.

Smith, F. (1994). *Understanding reading* (5th ed.). Hillsdale, NJ: Lawrence Erlbaum Associates.

Stahl, S. A. (1992). Saying the "p" word: Nine guidelines for exemplary phonics instruction. *The Reading Teacher, 45*, 618–625.

Stanovich, K. E. (1994). Romance and reality. *The Reading Teacher, 47,* 280–291.

Strickland, D. S. (1998). *Teaching phonics today: A primer for educators.* Newark, NJ: International Reading Association.

———. (1995). Reinventing our literacy programs: Books, basics, balance. *The Reading Teacher, 48,* 294–302.

Templeton, S. (1979). Spelling first, sound later: The relationship between orthography and higher order phonological knowledge in older students. *Research in the Teaching of English, 13,* 255–264.

Venezky, R. L. (1967). English orthography: Its graphical structure and its relation to sound. *Reading Research Quarterly, 2,* 75–106.

Weaver, C. (1990). *Understanding whole language: From principles to practice.* Portsmouth, NH: Heinemann Educational Books.

Yopp, H. K. (1992). Developing phonemic awareness in young children. *The Reading Teacher, 45,* 696–703.

Zuck, L. V. (1974). Some questions about the teaching syllabication rules. *The Reading Teacher, 27,* 583–588.

Zutell, J. (1979). Spelling strategies of primary school children and their relationship to Piaget's concept of decentration. *Research in the Teaching of English, 13,* 69–80.

8 - 17 - 2004

M D . U . S . A .